CONTENTS

004 / HIT THE STREETS

024 / TREASURE TROVE

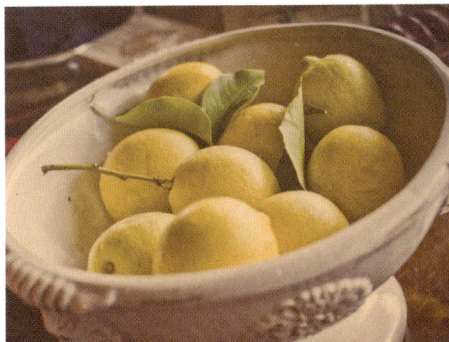

046 / FEELING PECKISH?

070 / NIGHT OWL

Truth: I first visited Perth in 2009 and was bored out of my mind. Sure, the beaches with their white sand and turquoise surf waters made Perth a traveller's paradise – if you prefer life in the slow lane – but where were the bars, where were the little cafes and, most importantly, where were the people after 5pm? Take two in 2011 and I've become one of Perth's biggest fans. Although this is the most isolated city in Australia, there are great experiences to be had if you only know where to go. It also helps that the city is undergoing a kind of transformation with new buildings popping up as fast as new reality shows on TV.

Hide & Seek Perth is for all locals, interstate travellers and overseas visitors who want to experience another side of what the city has to offer. We've done our best to identify 40 of the most interesting and unique places, both in the city centre and the 'burbs. The book is divided into four, colour-coded chapters packed with ideas to help you fill your day, your bag, your stomach and your ears: **HIT THE STREETS** (nine places to go or things to do once you've worked on your tan at the beach); **TREASURE TROVE** (ten unique shopping experiences that make you wonder why you bother with brand stores); **FEELING PECKISH?** (11 ways to fill your tummy by sampling Perth's eclectic range of eateries); **NIGHT OWL** (ten bars, clubs and music venues to get you glowing in the dark as you mingle, dance or groove the night away). There's something for everyone here, no matter what your tastes or interests. And, in all cases, we've tried to make sure that you won't go broke after one night out on the town.

I'd like to say thank you to the freelancers whose contributions have made this book possible: to Erika Budiman for her incredible design and excellent photographs, to Michelle Bennett for her editorial expertise, and to our in-house cartographer Emily Maffei for her funky maps. Thanks also to the amazing team of in-the-know local writers who researched and wrote the reviews with such enthusiasm and dedication.

Finally, if you find somewhere hidden in Perth that you think others should seek out, please send us an email at **info@exploreaustralia.net.au** or check out **www.hideseek.com.au** for more hidden places in cities around Australia. Otherwise, there are a couple of blank pages at the back of the book for you to record your own discoveries as you explore this truly accessible city.

Cheers,

Melissa Krafchek | Series editor

ABOUT THE WRITERS

JULIAN TOMPKIN

While earning his stripes – and staying out till all hours for far too many nights – documenting WA's much-lauded music scene over the past decade, Julian's insatiable passion for food and wine has taken him on some curious adventures into the nether regions of Perth's culinary soul. He likes it loud, hot, spicy and red, but isn't too fussy if it's your round.

EMMA BERGMEIER

A hunter of style who knows Perth's boutiques better than the back of her own hand, Emma loves local fashion, and isn't afraid to share her fashionable finds with everyone else. A stylist, blogger and journalist all rolled into one, Emma is passionate about supporting local designers and independent stores. Her blog is www.dropstitch.com.au, all about Perth street chic.

MAX VEENHUYZEN

Max is a freelance journalist who writes largely about food and drink for WA and national publications. From seeking out the city's best banh mi and Chinese barbecue dishes to saving his pennies for a seat at some of the world's best restaurants, enjoying and thinking about food occupies an inordinate amount of his life. He loves the cold weather and also drinks a lot of gin. Don't worry, the photo's just him as a kid – he's now above the legal drinking age.

CARMEN JENNER

Carmen is a born and bred Perth travel, food, and lifestyle writer. Her work has appeared in *Asian Geographic Passport*, in-flight magazines *Tiger Tales* and *Going Places*, *Chaat!* (the magazine for British Curry Club), *Cravings*, *The Australian* and the Perth edition of www.agendadaily.com. She has contributed to many Explore Australia guidebooks, including *Great Gourmet Weekends in Australia*. She is also a restaurant reviewer and writer for the *Top 50 Restaurant Guide WA*.

SARAH MCNEILL

Sarah drove across the Nullarbor to stay in Perth for 6 months – that was 25 years ago! She's an actor, arts editor and feature writer for a local Perth newspaper, covering all aspects of the arts. She and her actor husband are very involved in the thriving arts scene here, and believe it is getting more vibrant every year!

SAM WILSON

Sam is a Perth-born, but Melbourne-based, freelance writer and rock'n'roll tragic. She loves Perth primarily for its illustrious musical history and its indescribably sublime beaches, and always stocks up on Hogan's Chilli Sauce when she's in town.

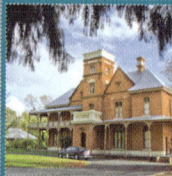

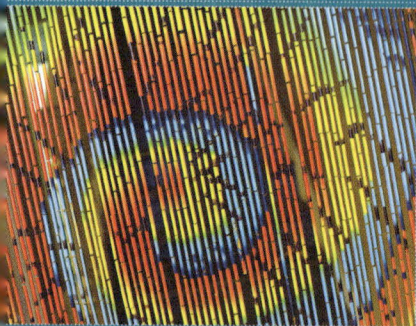

HIT THE STREETS

> HIT THE STREETS

THE BLUE ROOM THEATRE

UP-CLOSE AND PERSONAL PRODUCTIONS

Looking for theatre that's new, edgy and innovative? Don't want to worry about fancy glad rags or cardiac-arrest-inducing price tags? Then the Blue Room is the theatre for you. At the heart of the Perth Cultural Centre, nestled in amongst the big boys of the arts – the state's art gallery, library, and new multimillion-dollar theatre centre – the Blue Room is all about alternative independent theatre in a relaxed and sociable setting.

A creaky old building that was once a college science block is where you'll find an inexpensive bar and two small theatres run by the not-for-profit Performing Arts Centre Society. Grab a toasted sandwich and bevvy at the bar, then take your drink into either the main theatre, which seats 60, or the studio, seating 40. It's as intimate and casual as live theatre gets.

Shows might be provocative and confronting, hilarious, ridiculous, dramatic or experimental. All performances are self-produced by actors, writers, directors and managers who are dedicated to exploring new ideas. Those ideas may not always work, but they can always be refined and developed with audience interaction and feedback. Many of the shows are developed for the fringe-festival circuit and just as many get picked up by funded theatre companies for further development or touring.

Long before Perth even knew it had a cultural heart, the Blue Room was there making theatre. Seeing a show here provides an opportunity to be an integral part of the local, independent creative scene. Get along to the theatre and you're bound to see something inspiring, challenging and, above all, fun.

> **HIT THE STREETS**

53 James St, Northbridge
(08) 9227 7005
www.pacs.org.au
See website for show times and dates

See also
map 1 G3

> HIT THE STREETS

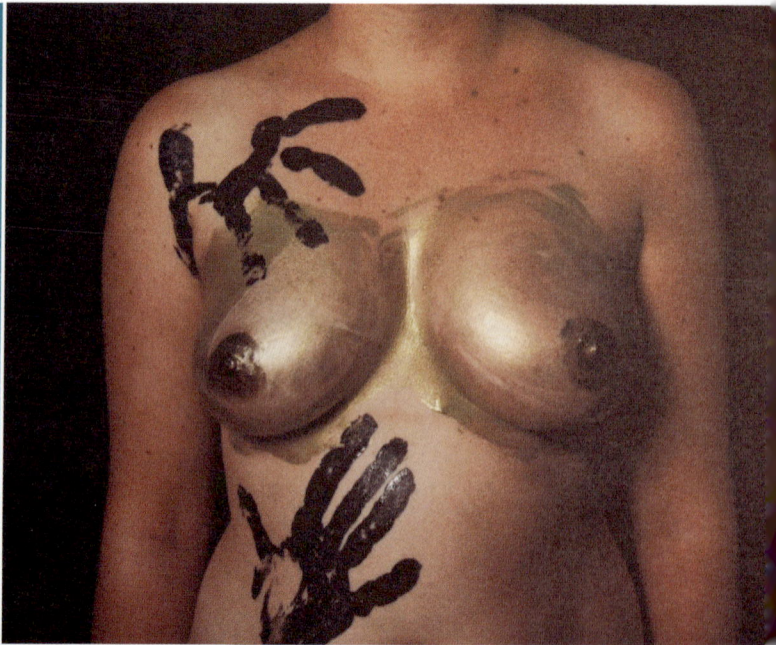

BREASTIQUE ART

FIND YOUR INNER BOOB ARTIST

Picture this: several topless women stand before canvases, mixing paints, chatting and musing over their prospective artwork. A buxom lass dips her nipple into crimson paint and, cupping her breast, applies the paint to her canvas with abandon. The next woman gets more tactile, smearing her breasts with paint, then smashing both boobs into the canvas.

No, this isn't happening at Hugh Hefner's mansion, but in a suburban garden with everyday women, some shapely, others lean; an expectant mum, a grandmother, a university student. It's an unlikely combo, but they all have one thing in common: supporting Breast Cancer Care WA, as the proceeds of these workshops are donated to the charity. Some of the women participating have been personally affected, while others come along for the fun of it, knowing it's for a worthy cause.

Breastique Art is the brainchild of Shiona Herbert, who had a flash of inspiration at a party when some of her bohemian friends whipped out their paints and body parts. Some of the paintings are conventional – fruit, flowers, trees – but the technique generally lends itself more to abstract shapes and forms. Experimentation is highly encouraged and it's not just canvases that are lavished with attention: clothing and household items are not safe (Shiona's fridge is truly a work of art) and even Barbie has been known to get in on the act.

Really, nothing is sacred when you gather a bunch of half-naked, invigorated, giggly women together.

> HIT THE STREETS

Location: Shiona runs Breastique Art wherever you desire
0408 173 669
www.breastiqueart.com

BON SCOTT PILGRIMAGE

IT'S A LONG WAY …

Western Australia certainly wasn't left wanting when it came to dishing out the natural wonders of the world: sublime beaches, immaculate weather … and AC/DC front man Bon Scott!*

As with Scott's musical narrative, this tour kicks off at the *North Fremantle Town Hall* ①. It was here Scott first cut his rock'n'roll teeth as a teenager, busting out some aural finery on the recorder. OK, not so rock'n'roll, but it wouldn't be long before the occasional bagpiper would be hitting the stages of Freo with his first band The Spektors.

Have a toast to Scott at *The Swan Hotel* ②, on the same street as the town hall and one place where Scott graced the stage, before making your way across the bridge and into Fremantle. Take a left down James Street (which becomes Ord Street) and you'll soon pass *John Curtin College* ③, the school where Scott would raise hell before bidding adieu at age 15 to hit the big stage with his breakthrough band The Valentines. Continue along Ord Street, then turn right onto Knutsford Street and left into Parry to *Fremantle Prison* ④, where a mischievous Scott would spend time for theft and being 'socially maladjusted'. Continue south down Parry Street and along *South Terrace* ⑤, a route well traversed by Scott from his days as the Freo post boy. Stroll left down Essex Street and across The Esplanade to the *Fishing Boat Harbour* ⑥ – where Scott would regularly report for duty throughout his teens aboard the throng of crayfish trawlers – and behold the *statue* ⑦ of the rock statesman standing loud and proud, complete with skin-tight jeans.

After toasting another ale to the loveable larrikin at *Little Creatures Brewery* ⑧, hail a cab and head for *Fremantle Cemetery* ⑨, where rock's greatest-ever front man is interred and awaiting your final salute.

> HIT THE STREETS

Starting point: North Fremantle Town Hall
222 Queen Victoria St, North Fremantle
End point: Fremantle Cemetery
Cnr Leach Hwy & Carrington St, Fremantle

See also

① map 2 B3
② map 2 B3
③ map 2 C4
④ map 2 B5
⑤ map 2 B5
⑥ map 2 B5
⑦ map 2 B5
⑧ map 2 B5
⑨ map 2 D4

'ENCYCLO' TRIVIA

* Indeed, the one-and-only Mr Bon Scott – whose golden tonsils fronted definitive Oz rockers AC/DC until his untimely death in 1980 – was proudly Western Australian.

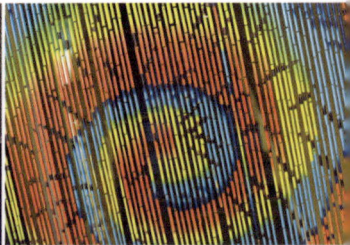

DR SNIPPY'S BARBER LOUNGE

SECRET MEN'S BUSINESS

Being a woman, I feel as though I've infiltrated a secret men's sanctuary as I sit in Dr Snippy's Barber Lounge waiting to chat with owner Clint Ariti. But Clint assures me I'm welcome and, given his charming demeanour, it seems a shame he doesn't handle the tresses of the fairer sex. Although, there's no need for him to expand the operation to include women: a loyal following of men ensures repeat business, with happy customers returning regularly for their bargain $27 haircuts ($24 if you're a student). Afternoons are particularly popular, when a free Coopers beer is thrown into the deal, but you can just walk in off the street without an appointment at any time of the day.

Chequered floors, comfy couches and a collection of other retro furniture from Clint's nan's house immediately relax even the most unmetrosexual of males. (The vintage paintings of fleshy babes in exotic locations help too.) It's a popular spot for rockabilly folk, who drop in for a quiff*, taper* or pompadour*. Flat tops, mohawks and those one-sided hairstyles so confusing to lovers of symmetry add pizzaz to the simple wash-and-trim requests of most blokes. Occasionally someone asks for a shave with a cut-throat razor, the mere mention of which sends shivers up the spines of other customers.

There's the added bonus of a free video game in the corner to keep patrons occupied while waiting – with the extra incentive of a gratis haircut if Clint's highest Pac-Man score of 294 260 is beaten. Although it's doubtful that anyone would be kept waiting that long, and even if they were, I doubt they would mind.

> **HIT THE STREETS**

204 Hay St, Subiaco
(08) 9381 3590
Open Tues–Wed 8am–6pm,
Thurs–Fri 10am–6pm, Sat 9am–3pm

See also
map 1 C3

'ENCYCLO' TRIVIA

* Quiff: Think of Elvis' crew cut and that forelock millions of women wanted to lovingly brush out of his eyes … or theirs!

* A taper is a crisp, short back and sides.

* A pompadour is like a quiff, only higher and without a parting. It was once favoured by medieval princesses who used to hide all kinds of items in their hair curls. Wonder what rockabillies hide in theirs?

PERTH CITY FARM

VEGGIES ARE OUR FRIENDS

When someone smiles at you and says, 'Of course your dog is welcome – would he like a bowl of water?', you know you're in the right place for a relaxed Saturday breakfast. Perth City Farm, a 'garden oasis in the middle of the concrete jungle', exudes the chilled and cheerful exuberance of people who know they're doing the right thing and are happy doing it.

With the dogs safely tied up, water bowls at the ready, their owners can happily browse the organic menu on the blackboard – no waste of paper or ink here – which promises free-range eggs and freshly picked herbs and veggies from the farm's own garden beds and chook pens. Breakfast delivers eggs scrambled with just-picked silverbeet, richly coloured with freshness, muesli with organic yoghurt and biodynamic boysenberries, homemade baked beans and still-warm muffins with organic coffee.

The small Saturday farmers' market sells ethical products and organic and biodynamic produce – which might cost a bit more than regular food, but hey, we'd rather pay for love and care than pesticides. A comprehensive permaculture nursery sells fruit trees, veggie seedlings, herbs and other plants.

Across the railway line from the CBD, City Farm originally started as a youth project so kids could learn that vegetables don't actually come wrapped in plastic. Community garden plots have taken off from there and there's also an experimental aqua farm.

Ride a bike, take public transport, walk (with Fido), or drive if you must, for a wholesome day down at the farm. What better way to start your day than with a little peace, love and brown rice?

> HIT THE STREETS

1 City Farm Pl, East Perth
(08) 9325 7230
www.perthcityfarm.org.au
Cafe open Mon–Fri 7am–2pm,
Sat 8am–12.30pm; Farmers' market
open Sat 8am–1pm

See also
map 1 I3

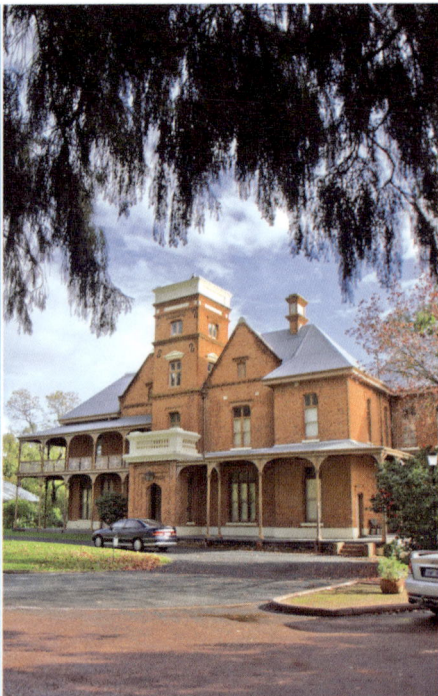

RIVERSIDE AT WOODBRIDGE

GRACE AND GRANDEUR ON A PLATE

It was never going to be easy to live out *Pride and Prejudice* fantasies on one of the driest, least-fertile continents on the planet. But Charles Harper tried his darndest to recreate the grandeur of Hertfordshire, and got pretty close. A 19th-century maverick, explorer, inventor, pastoralist, publisher, politician and gregarious chap, Harper was an entrepreneur who envisaged grand cities where there was little but swampy marshes and blood-thirsty mosquitoes.

In 1885 he built ye grand olde Woodbridge House, originally a Victorian-era manor, then a school for naughty children and later a nursing home (dozens of ghosts are said to roam its creaky hallways). One of Perth's few remaining manor houses rescued from breakneck development in the 1960s, this gracious relic has withstood Western Australia's rise, fall and rise again, all the time keeping watch over the meandering waters of the Swan River.

While it's a living museum of a very different Perth – the house is open for tours – it also boasts one of the city's finest country kitchens in the most spectacular of settings. Your granny's kitchen with million-dollar views, Riverside at Woodbridge is all about comfort food – homemade winter pies, Devonshire teas, Cornish pasties, Sunday roasts and old-fashioned cakes aplenty, along with loads of gluten-free options.

It also sits at the gateway to the Swan Valley, where some of the state's finest wineries, breweries and gastronomic artisans reside. Wine, beer and cheer await.

So slip into your finest threads and rekindle some old-world charm at this splendid spot, of which Mr Darcy would surely approve.

> **HIT THE STREETS**

8254 Ford St, Woodbridge
(08) 9274 1469
Open Mon–Tues & Thurs–Sun 9am–5pm

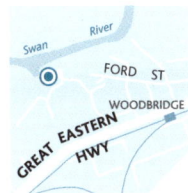

See also
map 3 C3

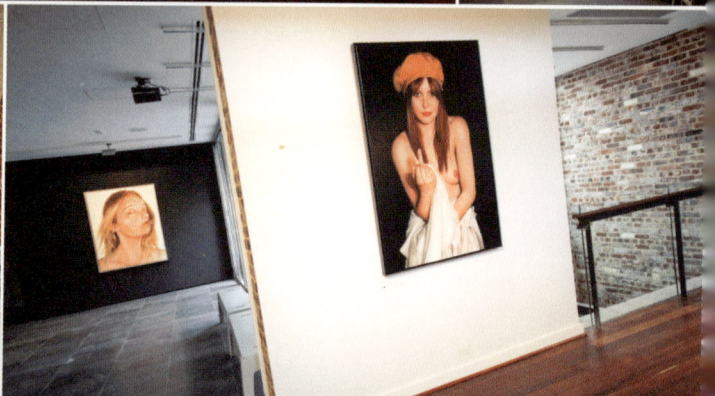

AN AUSSIE BITE OUT OF THE BIG APPLE

The word innovative is decidedly overused these days, but sometimes it's so fitting that to use another word would be resorting to your thesaurus just for the sake of it. VENN* is innovative with a capital 'I'. The first of its kind in Perth, this gallery/shop/bar/cafe/studio has injected more than a little life into the century-old flour mill in which it's housed.

VENN started out as a gallery with a retail component; this attracted such big crowds that the bar and cafe evolved to meet the demand. The gallery – where high-end design meets rustic studio – exhibits contemporary art and design, with artists showcasing their photographs, printmaking, paintings, drawings, sculptures and installation pieces.

Downstairs in the shop, sustainable products with refined design are the go, but there's also a playful element to them, like the ties woven from old cassette tapes, guaranteed to spice up the most staid business suit, or the crumpled city maps that save you from doing the crumpling yourself. Other items include beautiful books, gifts, jewellery and stationery.

The cafe serves breakfast through to dinner – from fluffy coconut pancakes to Fremantle sardines to seasonal tasting plates, coffee and cakes. It's standing room only on Friday nights, but there's plenty of breathing space upstairs on the roof terrace.

In the basement is where the serious stuff happens; here studios are available for artists to rent, to practise and cultivate their craft in a dynamic environment. The aim is to keep Perth artists local.

It's all very New York in both appearance and ideas, a concept as exciting – and innovative – as the city that never sleeps.

> HIT THE STREETS

16 Queen St, Perth
(08) 9321 8366
www.venn.net
Gallery open Tues–Thurs & Sat 10am–5pm, Fri 10am–7pm;
Shop open Mon–Thurs 9am–5pm, Fri 9am–8pm, Sat 10am–5pm;
Cafe/Bar open Mon–Tues 7am–5pm, Wed–Fri 7am–12am, Sat 9am–12am

See also
map 1 G4

'ENCYCLO' TRIVIA

* VENN is named after the Venn diagram, which, if you can remember back to Year 10 maths, is when circles overlap and their intersecting areas have something in common.

MACC COFFEE BAR & EVENTS

A FREE-SPIRITED FRINGE DWELLER

Like a grand utopian hippie commune plucked straight out of 1967 and transported to Fremantle aboard the acid mother ship, Macc Coffee Bar & Events is nothing if not unique – yet at the same time somehow manages to be typically Freo.

Located on the fringes of central Fremantle – in itself a statement – Macc is where art, food, coffee and the psychedelic meet. The converted warehouse space will have you constantly turning your head to check out music posters on the deck, clothing and art for sale next to the cafe, and crazy cactuses and a mishmash of second-hand furniture all around the place. It's a bit of a microcosm for Freo's contradictory essence, that heady mix of old-world charm versus cutting-edge artistic expression.

The kitchen is one of the most inspired in town (free-range Moroccan scrambled eggs anyone?) while also doubling as an artists' studio, home to many of Fremantle's finest established and emerging visual artists. Grab a house-blended coffee, which, incidentally is unbeatable (and that says a lot in a suburb prized for its reverence for the bean), and wander around watching art being made before your very eyes.

The venue operates as a cafe by day, marrying mostly European and South American flavours, then every Friday night the outdoor deck lights up and wood-fired pizzas are served, along with the sultry sounds of Western Australia's finest groove, folk and acoustic merchants of song.

So for an immaculate blend of coffee, food and inspiration dear freaked-out flower children, get on down and say hello to the free-spirited friendly folk at Macc.

> HIT THE STREETS

19 Blinco St, Fremantle
0433 486 923
www.maccoffee.com.au
Open Mon–Thurs & Sat–Sun 7am–3pm,
Fri 7am–10pm

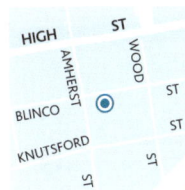

See also
map 2 C4

021

> HIT THE STREETS

MUSEUM OF PERFORMING ARTS

HIS MAJESTY'S SPECIAL COLLECTION

Long before the world discovered Lionel Logue in *The King's Speech**, theatre historian Ivan King was taking tours around His Majesty's Theatre, and talking about the speech therapist and actor who lived and performed in Perth before heading off to fame and fortune in London.

Lionel Logue is just one of a long string of famous directors, actors, dancers, singers and musicians who have graced the stage of 'The Maj' (as the theatre's affectionately known) since it opened in 1904, and who are now celebrated and immortalised at the theatre's Museum of Performing Arts (MOPA).

Former actor and director Ivan has been collecting theatrical memorabilia and ephemera for over 30 years. Upstairs he runs deliciously gossipy tours bringing life to the theatre's colourful show-biz history. Downstairs in the basement Ivan regularly changes MOPA's exhibitions, displaying his collection's amazing artefacts from some of the greatest names to have pirouetted and played across the stage.

For the price of a gold coin, you can see programs, posters, letters, photographs, press cuttings, costumes, scripts and scores that hark back to a golden era of theatre, dance, drama and marvellous musicals. See soprano Dame Nellie Melba's silk programs and prima ballerina Anna Pavlova's signed contract from when she toured Australia in 1926. Costumes include Dame Margot Fonteyn's tutu, Vivien Leigh's feather boa, Jill Perryman's red-sequinned dress from *Hello, Dolly!* and some of Dame Edna's fabulous frocks.

Even greats like Katharine Hepburn* have left reminders of their glamorous presence on Perth's main stage. Thanks to Ivan, you'll find it all downstairs at The Maj.

> HIT THE STREETS

Basement, His Majesty's Theatre,
825 Hay St, Perth
(08) 9265 0900
www.hismajestystheatre.com.au
Open Mon–Fri 10am–4pm

See also
map 1 F4

'ENCYCLO' TRIVIA

* Starring Colin Firth, the Oscar-winning film *The King's Speech* features Geoffrey Rush as Lionel Logue, the larrikin Aussie speech therapist who helped King George VI overcome his stammer when making public speeches.

* Hollywood legend Katharine Hepburn played Portia in *The Merchant of Venice*, performed in Perth in 1955.

TREASURE TROVE

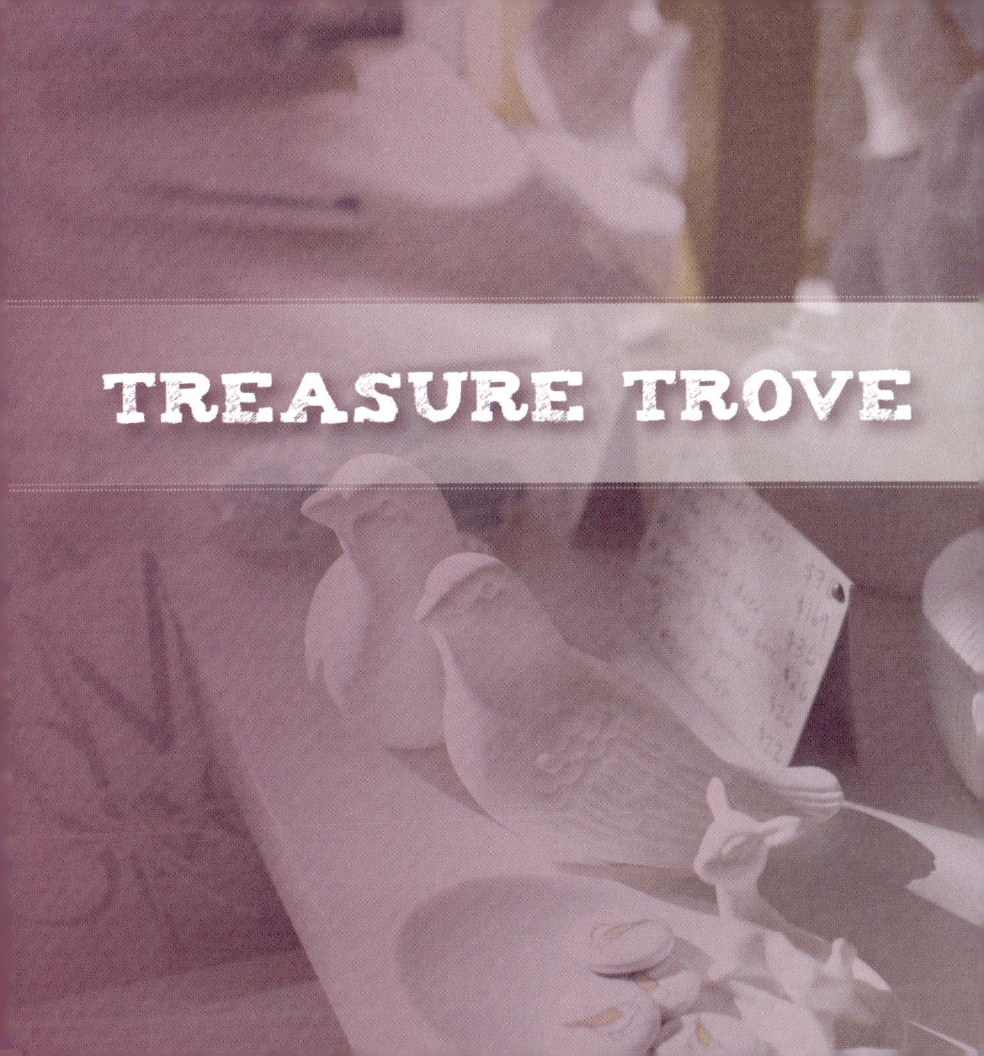

PIGEONHOLE

BIRDS OF A FEATHER SHOP TOGETHER

What's warm, friendly and more chirpy than a budgie at breakfast? The Pigeonhole empire, that's what, a flock of cute and tiny stores perched across Perth's CBD. Though every Pigeonhole store packs a big punch when it comes to character and personality, the shops themselves are diminutive in size, making for a cosy and memorable shopping experience.

The first Pigeonhole hatched at the end of the oft overlooked Bon Marche Arcade back in 2007. Since then, a further five stores have opened their doors, much to the delight of quirky camera coveters, fashion fiends and accessories aficionados.

A collection of international offerings awaits eagle-eyed shoppers who swoop into any of these delightful stores, with fashions from far-off locations such as Sweden and Finland, cameras from Tokyo and Korea, including cult photography brand Lomography, plus flock-loads of accessories designed right here in Australia. Pigeonhole is also home to products by The Impossible Project, a collective of former Polaroid employees based in Germany, who have kept the art of the Polaroid alive.

Every Pidge stocks a slightly different range of products, with Shop 9 in Shafto Lane brimming with wonderful women's fashion; Shop 7A in the same lane selling stationery, jewellery and goodies for little tackers; Shop 44 in London Court luring with cards, paper art and jewellery; the Fox Hunt at 220 William Street home to dapper menswear from across the globe; and the original Bon Marche Arcade nest (Shop 16) selling cameras, homewares, jewellery, fashion and art.

Whatever it is that gets your feathers pleasantly ruffled, the chirpy birds and boys at Pigeonhole have got you covered.

> TREASURE TROVE

Shop 16, Bon Marche Arcade,
80 Barrack St, Perth
(08) 9221 9837
Open Mon–Thurs & Sat 10.30am–5.30pm,
Fri 10.30am–8pm

Shop 7A & Shop 9, Shafto La,
401 Murray St, Perth
(08) 9321 8112 & (08) 9322 3430
Open Mon–Thurs & Sat 10.30am–5.30pm,
Fri 10.30am–8pm
www.pigeonhole.com
(see website for other locations)

See also
map 1 G4

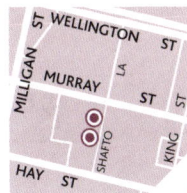

See also
map 1 F4

> TREASURE TROVE

OH HENRY! VINTAGE

FASHION TO WALK THE PLANK FOR

Ahoy there! Are you tired of searching the seven seas for affordable vintage treasure? Well you can breathe a sigh of relief, me hearties, coz Oh Henry! Vintage has washed ashore. Heaving with a bounty of second-hand fashions for buccaneers and sea-faring lasses*, this nautical-styled gem – think lashings of rope, weathered wood and other seafaring gear – is worth its weight in gold.

Oh Henry's captain, the adventurous Miss Jasmine, travels the world in search of vintage loot, and she sure has unearthed a lot of it, with fashions from the 1940s through to the '90s stocked in her store. Scale the rickety stairs up to the crow's nest, drop anchor and be rewarded with a range of beautiful frocks (in every colour of the rainbow), fascinators, suits, sunglasses, retro Ts and more, all affordably priced so you don't have to blow all your doubloons* to walk away with something dandy.

Seagoing scenesters who favour one particular colour will give the layout here top marks, as every piece of clothing is grouped with similar shades. Finding yourself a purple party frock, a neat navy blazer, a glamorous green maxi dress or a slinky black number has never been so easy. If pre-loved fashion is your booty of choice, there's simply no sailing past Oh Henry!

> TREASURE TROVE

Level 1, 242 William St, Northbridge
(enter from Francis St)
(08) 9328 9891
Open Tues–Sat 10.30am–5.30pm,
Sun 12–4.30pm

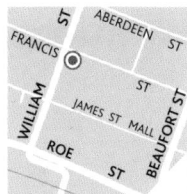

See also
map 1 G3

'ENCYCLO' TRIVIA
* Fear not, landlubbers: you'll also love the vintage gear on offer here.

* Doubloons are Spanish gold coins collected by pirates …

WILLIAM TOPP

FOR THE LITTLUN WITHIN

If curiosity does in fact kill cats, then felines (and crazy cat ladies) are warned to steer well clear of William Topp. A purveyor of curios and bric-a-brac from here, there and everywhere, William Topp is a charming homewares and accessories store that has nothing you need but everything you want.

With thousands of products occupying every nook and cranny, a visit to William Topp has the power to wake up the child within, sparking a sense of curiosity and vivaciousness that many of us lose once we've grown up (or at least think we have).

Stepping through the red doors you'll discover treasure more glistening than Ariel's secret cave in *The Little Mermaid*. Look to the left and there's jewellery and accessories galore, or step to the right to get hands on with stamp sets, hanging mobiles, robot toys and other bits and bobs. The huge selection of jewellery and accessories includes such lovelies as hand-knitted scarves and beanies from Melbourne knitting royalty Otto + Spike, and ceramic necklaces from Portuguese sister duo Braille.

Other coveted items designed to make home and life more beautiful and fun include Pantone* mugs, Pac-Man cookie cutters and Third Drawer Down* tea towels. If your home is already chock-a-block with first-hand homewares, take the time to peruse the carefully selected range of re-found items, such as ceramic plates and vases, that owner Kate has collected over the years.

Next time your home or wardrobe – or your relationship with your inner child – is in need of a shake up, leave the kitty committee at home and pounce on William Topp.

> TREASURE TROVE

452 William St, Northbridge
(08) 9228 8733
www.williamtopp.com
Open Tues–Fri 11am–6pm,
Sat 11am–5pm, Sun 11am–4pm

See also
map 1 H2

'ENCYCLO' TRIVIA

* The authority on colour for graphic designers and artists, Pantone produces a rainbow of computer-friendly shades. These mugs allow the colour conscious to adorn their morning cuppa with their favourite tone.

* A collective of design-conscious individuals based in Melbourne, Third Drawer Down produces and curates a range of items that feature artwork from illustrators and designers.

TEA FOR ME

FANCY A CUPPA CHA?

'Picture you upon my knee, just tea for two, and two for tea …' So go the lyrics from 'Tea for Two'*, a song from a bygone era that seems fitting as you enter the specialty tea shop Tea for Me – after all, we all know that rituals like tea drinking are much better shared.

The first thing you'll likely notice in amongst all the boxes of tea leaves is the intoxicating earthy aromas of 100+ tea flavours, including such current favourites around town as soursop green tea. To mention the other flavours might give away the highly guarded catalogue (sounds rather cloak and dagger-ish, but competition is fierce in the tea industry …), so a visit to one of the two Tea for Me stores is the best way to discover just how many ways the humble tea leaf can be dressed up.

What we can tell you is that there's a tea for pretty much whatever ails you: immune boosters, skin purifiers, calming herbal infusions. No wonder tea enthusiasts travel from all over the state to replenish their supplies, and it's the tea of choice for numerous eateries around Perth.

Proprietor Barry Dawson sources his tea in a very hands-on way – no agents or packing houses for him. He travels to countries such as China, India and Sri Lanka, visiting small farms that preserve traditional cultivating methods, and taste-testing every single variety.

So next time you fancy sharing a nice hot cuppa, before you put the kettle on, drop in to Tea for Me (and you).

> TREASURE TROVE

Shop 3, 94 Rokeby Rd, Subiaco
(08) 9380 9377
Open Mon–Fri 9.30am–5pm,
Sat 9am–4pm

20A London Crt, Perth
(08) 9221 7175
Open Mon–Fri 9am–5pm
www.teaforme.com.au

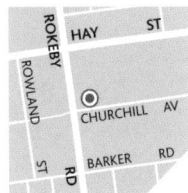

See also
map 1 B4

See also
map 1 G4

'ENCYCLO' TRIVIA
* 'Tea for Two' is a song from the 1925 musical *No, No, Nanette*.

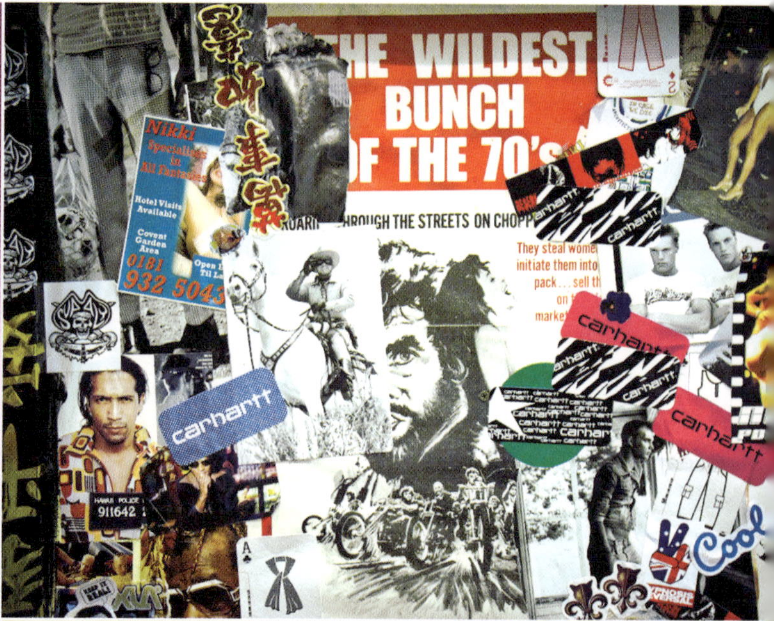

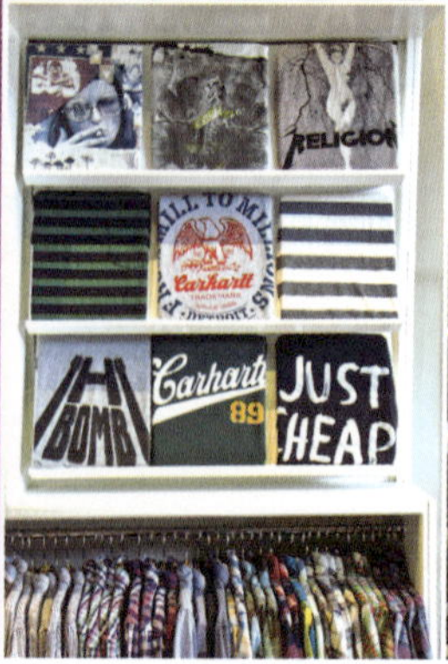

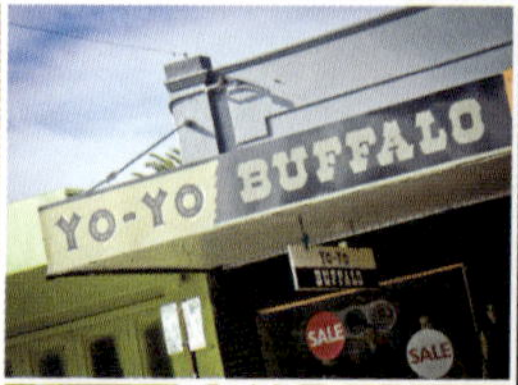

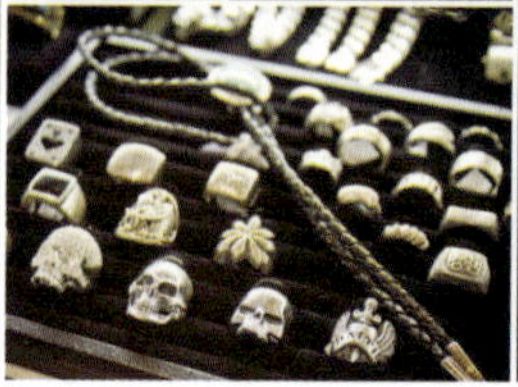

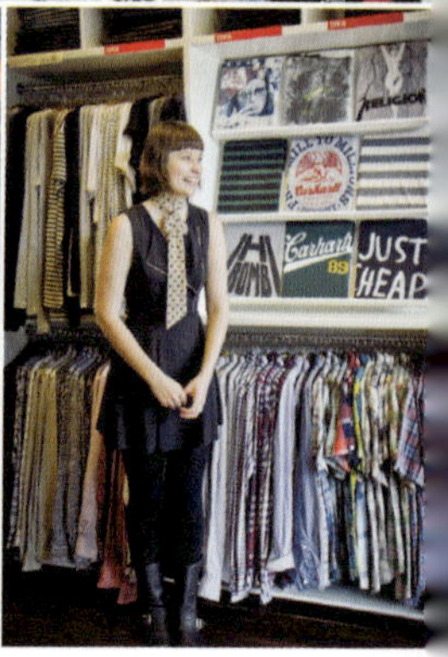

> TREASURE TROVE

YO YO BUFFALO

RIDE 'EM, COWBOY!

There once was a time – a while back, but still within living memory – when Perth was better known for its provinciality than its 'fabulosity'. Things are different now, of course, but those of us who remember the 'big country town' years will be forever grateful to Yo Yo Buffalo for helping usher in a brave new era of rock'n'roll chic.

Since setting up shop on West Leederville's happening Oxford Street strip in 1994, this little boutique has kept the city's hepcats and kittens looking sharp in indie designer clothing, personality-plus accessories and stylin' footwear. Make no mistake: Yo Yo Buffalo is *c-o-o-l*. But it's also friendly and fun, with attitude-free staff and prices to suit most budgets.

Describing itself as 'small but perfectly formed', Yo Yo sure manages to maximise its minimal dimensions. Dreaming of the perfect pair of jeans? You've come to the right place: cult brands like Cheap Monday, G-Star and NEUW number among the store's denim delights. Unabashedly girly vintage frocks share rack space with edgier, fashion-forward numbers; British rock Ts and soul-boy shirts rub shoulders with mod-inspired jackets. As if that's not reason enough to try something on, the change rooms are a drawcard in themselves, their walls lovingly collaged with old magazine photos, stickers and band flyers.

But the real ace up Yo Yo Buffalo's sleeve? Unique accessories that'll get you noticed without walloping your wallet. Choose from Native American jewellery or sassy rockabilly baubles, flamboyant cowboy boots or sunnies fit for a Hollywood starlet: there's bound to be something with your name on it.

And that, amigos, is nothing less than yo-yo fantastico!

> **TREASURE TROVE**

134 Oxford St, West Leederville
(08) 9443 4774
Open Mon & Sat 10am–5pm, Tues–Wed
& Fri 10am–6pm, Thurs 10am–9pm,
Sun 11am–5pm

See also
map 1 D1

> TREASURE TROVE

FEATHER YOUR NEST

If you're a hoarder trying to cull your possessions, it would pay to listen to the wise person who once said, 'only keep something if it's useful, beautiful or has sentimental value … Oh, and stay away from shops like Mr Sparrow.' When visiting this delightful 'home, gift and garden' store, you'll almost certainly leave with a collection of pretty things you'll find hard to ever part with.

Much like its namesake, the shop is tiny but with plenty to admire. Upon entering Mr Sparrow's nest, you'll realise this ain't no ordinary gift shop when you spy the whimsical bath tub water feature. Owner Anna Macoboy sources a unique mix of new, handmade, designer and second-hand goodies from all corners of the globe, including the big cyberspace in the sky. Her treasures will leave a trail of loveliness throughout your home, from the kitchen to the living room, passing by your wardrobe into the office, and out into the garden – where you may even attract a sparrow of your own with one of the bird feeders.

Sure, Mr Sparrow stocks some practical items like gardening gloves, scarves, teapots, notebooks and beautiful stationery. But it's the playful items that really charm, like the upside-down planters (ideal for growing gravity-defying herbs in your kitchen), the sparrow-shaped pegs, the egg pants (not the vegetable, but egg cups shaped as trousers) and cute dishes that resemble buttons.

Just be warned. Mr Sparrow is a bit like a toy boy (or bird) on the arm of his latest squeeze: he's there to enchant and delight, and fly away with your imagination if you don't hold on tight.

> TREASURE TROVE

Shop 3, 223 Bagot Rd, Subiaco
(08) 9381 6362
www.mrsparrow.com.au
Open Mon–Wed & Fri 9.30am–5.30pm,
Thurs 9.30am–7pm, Sat 10am–5pm

See also
map 1 B4

> TREASURE TROVE

THE PEARL OF HIGHGATE

THE GREAT AUSSIE PIE ... WITH A TWIST

Once a proud example of Australia's culinary fortitude, the humble meat pie has taken a back seat of late, resigned to lukewarm bains-marie in suburban delicatessens. But it's a different story altogether at the Pearl of Highgate, a backstreet bakery where pies have always taken centre stage.

The Pearl is an obsession for some and a revelation for most, unlikely in oh-so-many ways. A maverick in the ever-gentrified surrounds of Highgate, this little shopfront has reinvigorated an age-old baking tradition with a dash of daring and a pantry packed with flavours from the furthest reaches of the globe. Don't let the unassuming exterior fool you – the Pearl of Highgate well and truly lives up to its grandiose moniker.

The humble pie has never tasted so damn glorious, especially when prefixed with such delectable companions as lamb and mint chutney, macadamia and parmesan, beef rendang*, and beef and chilli goulash. In bringing together the patisserie smarts of central Europe and a good ol' Aussie baking tradition, this place has catapulted the pie into the 21st century, while retaining its proud and humble roots as an affordable and satisfying meal.

While it's the pie that reigns supreme here, this bakery doesn't flounder when it comes to the sweeter side of life. From delicate walnut gugelhupf* to luscious panforte* and pecan-and-fig tarts, there is something to complement even the most obscure of pies.

The good folk here have always known that no one wants to eat humble pie, so they've elevated these babies to stratospheric culinary heights. You need never go near a bain-marie again.

> TREASURE TROVE

189 Lincoln St, Highgate
(08) 9228 9011
Open Tues–Fri 7am–4pm,
Sat–Sun 7am–1pm

See also
map 1 H1

'ENCYCLO' TRIVIA

* Rendang is a dry and spicy coconut curry.

* Gugelhupf is a marble cake with a distinctive ring shape that has its origins in Germany, Austria and Switzerland.

* Panforte is a classic Italian cake that's dense and chewy and contains dried fruit and nuts.

BEYOND SKATE

THE DAILY GRIND

Every weekday in the middle of Perth's grey CBD, hundreds of briefcase-toting individuals dash past a little store flanked by dreary high-rise buildings that are home to accounting firms, banks and the like. These suit-sporting men and women are in such a rush, they never even notice the sub-cultural oasis that is Beyond Skate. But for dexterous peeps who grind* around the city on a wooden deck, the store is a hot spot for fashion, culture and skater supplies.

It's on weekends when the shop comes into its own: this is when skaters come out to play, taking advantage of the empty footpaths and deserted streets, before kickflipping* in to Beyond to hang out and peruse decks and fashions from Australia and beyond.

It may be home to skate-centric labels such as Supply, Butter Goods, Mr Simple, GMTA, 10.Deep and Monster Children, but Beyond isn't just for skaters, with plenty of books, art and other goodies to appease those who aren't coordinated enough to get around town on a small slab of Canadian maple. There's also a coveted wall of shoes on offer, with Vans, Nike and adidas sneakers available in every imaginable colour.

Though it's a specialty retailer, staff at Beyond are friendly, approachable and knowledgeable, welcoming all and sundry into their small but sensational store. Whether you ride switch*, goofy* or just get around town on foot, you're bound to find something above and beyond the norm.

> TREASURE TROVE

15 Howard St, Perth
(08) 9481 2299
www.beyondskate.com
Open Mon–Thurs 10am–6pm,
Fri 10am–8.30pm, Sat 9am–5pm,
Sun 12–5pm

See also
map 1 G4

'ENCYCLO' TRIVIA

* Grinding is when you scrape a board's axles on a curb or railing.

* The kickflip is a classic skateboarding manoeuvre, where the rider flips the board over in the air.

* Riding switch means you stand facing the opposite direction to usual.

* Someone who rides goofy has their left foot at the back of their board.

RED DUSK DESIGNS

FEMME FATALE WEAR

Your curves are so dangerous they need restraining, your lethal waist cinched-in so tightly that your breasts have no choice but to heave. You've been seduced by corsetry, titillated by burlesque and you can flutter your eyelashes with the best of them. But the most important question any femme fatale asks is, 'What to wear?' You could slink into an adult shop, but why not opt for a more personalised approach and make an appointment with Red Dusk Designs?

Owner Jolieske Loosjes sources beautiful vintage and burlesque-inspired treasures from all around the world, specialising in bustiers and steel-boned corsets – guaranteed to inspire all kinds of bodice-ripping scenarios. Other items to add to your dress-up box include feathered angel wings, '50s-style cat-eye glasses, cigarette holders, tassel pasties and sexy stockings. More sensible days call for cropped jackets, woollen coats, platform shoes and boots, and tailored or petticoat skirts that team beautifully with a corset or bustier. And ladies needn't miss out on dressing up their men, with cufflinks, ties and gangster braces also available.

Then there are the steampunk*-inspired timepieces that can be worn as necklaces, around your wrist or whipped out of your pocket (you just never know when a dashing suitor might request the time). Jolieske also sells exquisite jewellery, masks and headwear that she designs and handcrafts herself. She keeps prices down by operating from her North Perth home; pieces range from $12 for an eye mask to around $200 for a corset. Just be warned: many a seductress has been seduced by Red Dusk Designs.

> ## > TREASURE TROVE

Address details provided when you make an appointment through the website
www.redduskjewellery.com
Open by appointment

'ENCYCLO' TRIVIA

* Steampunk is a trend inspired by the Industrial Revolution that focuses on structured lines, buckles, brass and military-meets-Mad-Max.

NELL'S EMPORIUM

A PASSION FOR FASHION AND FOOD

Most fashion folk in the know are used to seeing designer extraordinaire Fenella Peacock taking a bow at the end of a catwalk. But now they're just as likely to find her dressed to the nines cooking in the kitchen at Nell's Emporium, a hybrid cafe and boutique she created to satisfy two passions in one.

From having her own label, Empire Line, back in the 1980s to joining the famed Ant!podium* team, Fenella has always worked in fashion, presenting 'tongue-in-chic' designs that are playful and cheeky but always stylish. Now you can find her creations at Nell's, housed in an old cottage on a quiet leafy street, with garments from Fenella's self-titled label, plus Ant!podium collections, TotoMoto* jewellery and a few other hand-picked pieces from Fenella's favourite local designers.

But it's behind the boutique where the magic really happens: sliding French doors open onto a sun-drenched courtyard cafe, where Fenella, smiling from ear to ear and wearing the latest threads from her own collections, dishes up mouth-watering rustic treats that fill the belly and warm the soul. Think baked eggs with leeks and truffle, lemonade infused with rose water, and a variety of warming soups and fresh salads.

Has she possibly been hanging out with that other stylish queen of the kitchen? We think so. Fusing food, fashion and fun with fabulous results, Fenella could easily give Nigella a run for her money.

> TREASURE TROVE

17 Glyde St, Mosman Park
(08) 9418 8863
Open Mon–Sat 9.30am–5pm

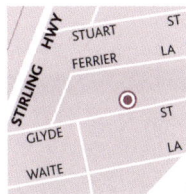

See also
map 2 B1

'ENCYCLO' TRIVIA

* Offering up coveted designs since 2003 and one of the most respected cult labels on the Australian fashion scene, Ant!podium is the brainchild of Fenella, her sister Ashe Peacock and Geoffrey Finch.

* Based in Perth, TotoMoto produces eye-catching jewellery in luscious gold tones that often features critters such as beetles and birds.

FEELING PECKISH?

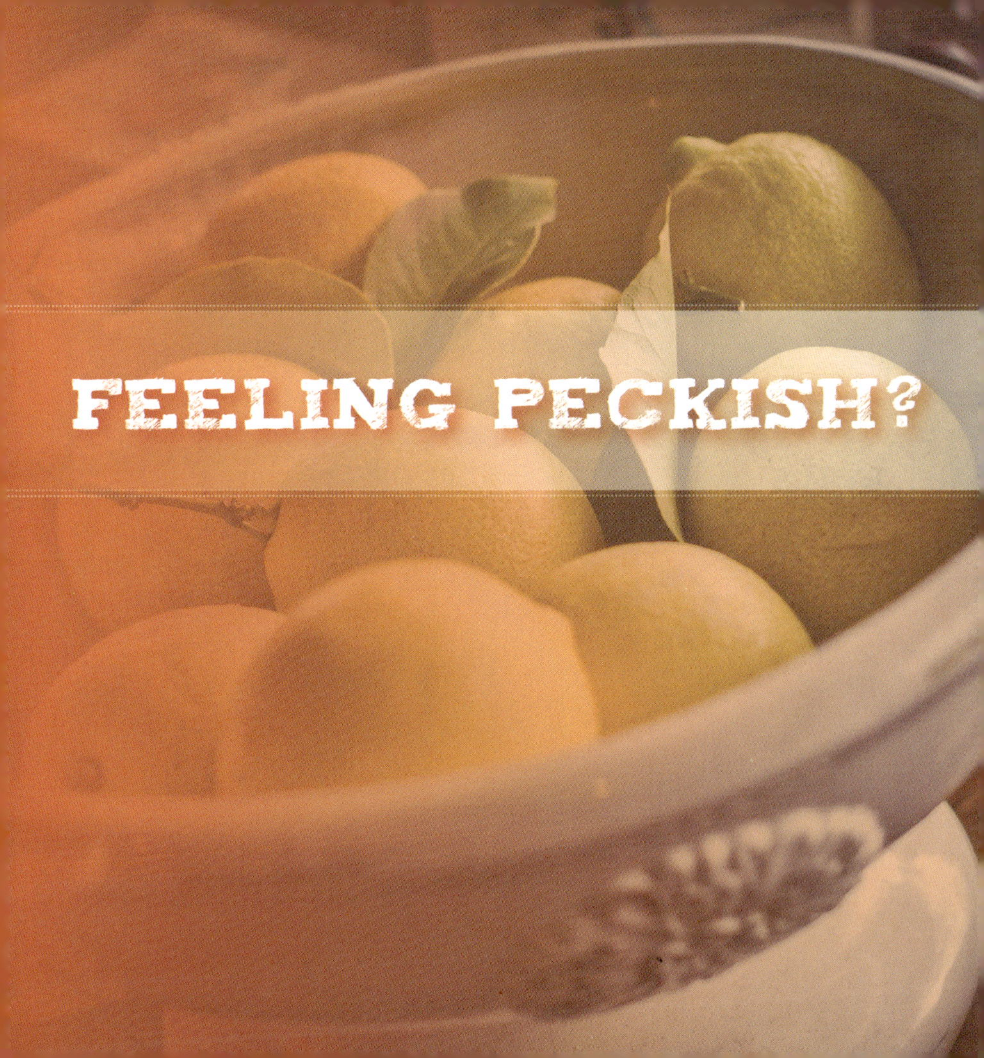

For those who like their coffee down a laneway, through a carpark, in a stable.

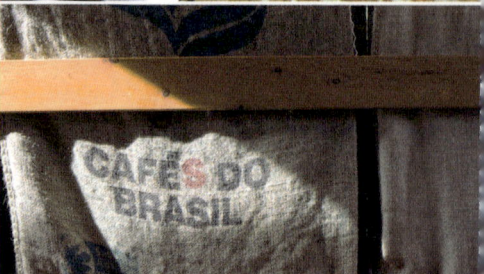

> FEELING PECKISH?

A BEAST OF A COFFEE DEN

Coffee is serious business at Pony Express O. So serious that the cafe has gone all out on its most vital piece of equipment, investing in the undisputed king of all coffee machines, the Slayer*, which retails for a whopping $30 000. You see, Pony Express O's brews aren't just something you mindlessly slam back in the morning to help get your brain into gear. No, they're *the* prime reason to get out of bed – each cup is a work of art that has to be tasted to be believed.

In an odd little building behind bustling Hay Street, this rustic space was established over 100 years ago as a stable to service the horses of businesspeople coming in and out of town. These days, the Slayer, Pony's friendly staff and the cafe's unpretentious and inviting atmosphere draw in countless coffee connoisseurs. The interior layout is quite unusual, with baristas standing side-by-side with customers while their drinks are being made, providing a perfect opportunity for hardcore coffee fans to pick the brains of those in the know.

There's one thing and one thing only on the minds of staff at Pony Express O and that's coffee – the cafe doesn't bother selling anything that doesn't come out of the Slayer, so punters are encouraged to BYO breakfast or lunch to nibble on while sipping away on their perfect cup of Joe. So saddle up your sandwich bags, jump aboard your steed and giddy up!

> FEELING PECKISH?

21 Mayfair St, Perth
0412 924 434
Open Mon–Fri 7am–3pm

See also
map 1 D3

'ENCYCLO' TRIVIA

* I mean, really, who's gonna argue with a coffee made by 'the Slayer'?

WHERE THERE'S SMOKE …

There are two certainties when it comes to cook-your-own Korean: firstly, you're going to be eating a lot of meat, and secondly, you're going to smell of smoke and pork fat. Not such a good look – or more appropriately, scent – if you're planning to paint the town red. The solution? Make Tong86, a Korean barbecue joint, the final rather than first stop on your night out in Northbridge.

To help ease the transition from beats to eats, there's a clubby, warehouse-dance-party vibe to Tong's high-ceilinged, ever-so-slightly industrial dining room, where the walls are decorated with graffiti and high-energy K-pop* video projections. While Korean booze such as soju* and Hite beer are available for those not quite ready to call it a night, most come here for the pork and beef, ordered by the well-priced plateful, that you barbecue yourself at your table.

In addition to familiar cuts, such as scotch fillet and pork belly, lesser seen ones (intestine, neck, intercostals*) should appease the adventurous eater, as will the 'worm soup' (we'll spare you the details, however, we can assure you that this dish's earthy flavour has nowt to do with your common garden-variety earthworm).

Of course, a Korean meal just wouldn't be complete without all those fun little side dishes, including the ubiquitous kimchi*. Also fun are the under-table buttons used to grab the staff's attention – as well as allow you to recreate your favourite Mr-Burns-and-Homer moment from *The Simpsons* to hilarious effect.

This is food best eaten communally and with abandon, so assemble the posse, order up big and don't forget to stop by the convenience store on your way home for a bottle of shampoo.

> FEELING PECKISH?

86 Beaufort St, Northbridge
(08) 9227 6006
Open Mon–Thurs 5pm–12am,
Fri–Sat 5pm–1am, Sun 5–10pm

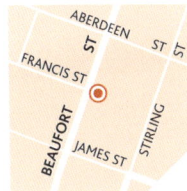

See also
map 1 H3

'ENCYCLO' TRIVIA

* Familiar with the saccharine-sweet strains of Japanese pop music, aka J-Pop? Meet its cousin from across the Korea Strait, Korean pop.

* Soju is a Korean distilled beverage that tastes like sweetened vodka. It's usually drunk neat.

* Intercostals is the meat between the short ribs of a cow.

* Kimchi is the name given to Korea's fermented vegetable dishes. There are loads of different varieties, however, cabbage usually features prominently. It's almost always spicy, and almost always addictive.

> FEELING PECKISH?

ALFRED'S KITCHEN

PUTTING THE BEEF BACK IN BURGER

After a decade in the sin bin, the burger's finally back on trend. Mind you, at Alfred's Kitchen it never went out of fashion. Indeed, for the best part of 70 years, Alf's – as it's colloquially known – has been dishing up the most celebrated burgers in the eastern suburbs, and beyond. While the makeshift caravan has long since been replaced by a permanent brick structure, Alfred's retains its rustic allure – it's little more than a kitchen and a counter, a few open-air benches and a roaring fire to warm the cockles.

In the pantheon of burgers, the jaw-lockers you get here are the real deal, bundles of down-to-earth goodness that hark back to another time, with not a gluten-free ciabatta or organic grain-fed patty to be found. Alfred's is a shrine to the burger of yesteryear, where salad is a fancy word for onion, lettuce and tomato, eggs are on the sunny side, cheese is yellow and condiments are a swig of Worcestershire sauce on your bun … if you're feeling a tad posh, that is.

Boasting a menu of 40 burgers – of which the most legendary remain the award-winning and multi-storeyed Cram, and Alfred's Special* – this place is so dedicated to its culinary tradition it could well be mistaken for retro. But fear not fashion adversaries: denim and meat still rule in these parts*.

As the world of food gets more complex, Alfred's Kitchen is a rare soul – a tribute to a culinary art that has been all but pillaged by negligible fast-food chains and fashionista burger bars. Reclaim the burger!

> **FEELING PECKISH?**

Cnr Meadow & James sts, Guildford
(08) 9377 1378
www.alfredskitchen.com.au
Open Sun–Thurs 5pm–1am,
Fri–Sat 5pm–3am

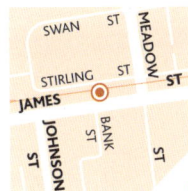

See also
map 3 A4

'ENCYCLO' TRIVIA

* Alfred's Special (pictured) is all about bacon, egg, pickle, lettuce, tomato and cheese on toasted bread, while the Cram packs a beef patty, beef steak, bacon, egg, cheese and salad into a bun.

* Although vegetarians can also rejoice, with the option of either a lentil or veg burger … yum!

TOAST

A WINNER, ANY WAY YOU SLICE IT

'Bashed-up French seaside' is how Ursula Rose, the owner of Toast, describes her cafe perched on the water's edge at Claisebrook Cove. The French Riviera has come to town, albeit a rustic Aussie version.

Ursula set out to create a place that feels like it's been there forever – and she succeeded. Open only a couple of years, the retro cafe has an energetic flow, welcoming everyone from suits to families to the lycra-clad drinking coffee from mismatched china. As you'd expect, the cafe's namesake appears prominently on the menu, with loads of doughy delights: from sourdough white to potato-and-parmesan toast, polenta bread to challah*. Toppings include Nutella, banana and cinnamon sugar, and, of course, Vegemite.

If you'd prefer to go beyond bread, try the corn fritters and bacon drizzled with maple syrup, or perhaps the delish rhubarb crepe with raspberry compote and toasted almonds. All the cakes, muffins and biscuits are baked on site, and there are gluten-free options. It's all hearty and honest food in a prime location – which, incidentally, isn't reflected in the cafe's prices. Overlooking the water, patrons always have something to admire, from the passing parade of sailing vessels to the surrounding multilevel designer abodes.

Keeping things simple is another of Toast's secrets: it's not over-stylised, you order at the counter and bookings aren't taken. Did we mention the drenching year-round sunshine? Yep, another advantage of that prime waterside posi. We propose a toast to Toast!

> **FEELING PECKISH?**

Shop 21, 60 Royal St, East Perth
(08) 9221 0771
www.toasteastperth.com
Open Mon–Sun 7am–7pm

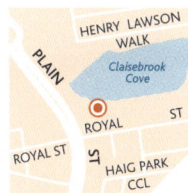

See also
map 1 J3

'ENCYCLO' TRIVIA

* Challah is a traditional Jewish eggy bread that's usually braided; it's a bit like a brioche.

GOOD ONE BBQ RESTAURANT

TRUTH IN ADVERTISING

There's something endearing about the way the Chinese christen their restaurants. You could almost design a set of dice for would-be restaurateurs to roll when brainstorming a name. Golden Dragon Century Phoenix Lucky Fortune anyone? But while Good One kowtows to Chinese eating-house naming conventions, it isn't afraid to rage against the machine either.

First of all, it resides in Victoria Park and not the Chinese barbecued-meat hot spot that is Northbridge. And secondly, it rocks hard. From juicy, bright-red char siu* to fat chunks of roast pork that are crunchy, salty and juicy all at once, Chinese barbecue greatness is Good One's calling card. Owner Wah Fung has been roasting and chopping since childhood – that he still has all 10 fingers says much about his dexterity with a cleaver.

While Mr Wah's chop shop sits front and centre, a kitchen at the back is called upon regularly for tabletop support, its arsenal covering everything from mainstream Asian – honey king prawns, say, or fiery Szechuan chicken – to lesser known yet equally delicious combinations like beef with winter melon. Whatever takes your fancy, it's worth knowing that the salt-and-pepper anything is a shoo-in for satisfaction. And dining with a tribe means more dishes and more variety: think of it as playing a culinary *Wheel of Fortune* with your table's lazy Susan, only everyone's a winner!

As if prices weren't reasonable enough, BYO means boo-yah when it comes to budgeting, although on occasion some high-profile chefs have been spied uncorking some big-ticket bottles. But really, it matters little if you're popping Moët or swigging Moselle, every (good) one is a winner here.

> FEELING PECKISH?

808 Albany Hwy, East Victoria Park
(08) 9472 4354
Open Wed–Mon 12–10pm

See also
map 1 J5

'ENCYCLO' TRIVIA

* Char siu is Chinese barbecued pork fillet, marinated in a sweet and salty sauce that usually includes five-spice, sugar and salt, although the spice mix varies from roaster to roaster. It's often coloured bright red and found hanging in restaurant windows.

SCANDINAVIA MEETS DOWNTOWN PERTH

Ever dreamt of escaping the city madness in favour of a cosy log cabin somewhere? Well, at Cabin Fever you don't even have to leave town: with wood panelling galore and an assortment of cuckoo clocks, bric-a-brac and mismatched crockery, you'll feel like you've landed in some Scandinavian doll's holiday house.

In true log-cabin form, this cute little cafe champions steaming hot drinks, serving up every kind of tea imaginable* on more second-hand teacups and saucers than you can poke a vintage teaspoon at (and there are plenty of those on hand, should you wish to do so). Being the tastiest member of the Pigeonhole* family, the friendly staff also dish up lots of hearty homemade grub: think yummy muffins and other baked treats, classic toasted sandwiches, quiches, steaming-hot soups and the like. Everything's served on vintage plates, which accentuates the Cabin's quirky charm even more.

Cabin Fever is also a makeshift art gallery, with work from local artists adorning the walls (in amongst all those cuckoo clocks and wooden owls), so you can soak up some culture with your cuppa.

Much cheaper than a trip to northern Europe and with way less snow to contend with (none in fact), a trip to Cabin Fever will warm the cockles of your heart and cure any get-out-of-town urges in a flash.

> FEELING PECKISH?

Shop 12, Bon Marche Arcade,
80 Barrack St, Perth
(08) 6142 6961
www.pigeonhole.com
Open Mon–Fri 7am–4pm,
Sat 10am–4pm

See also
map 1 G4

'ENCYCLO' TRIVIA

* Choose from teas like 'liquorice legs', Turkish apple and China jasmine.

* A family of independent stores scattered across Perth, Pigeonhole is home to all things cute, quirky and unusual, with fashion, photography, art, homewares and more. See the review on p. 27.

CLANCY'S FISH PUB

JUST WHAT THE DOCTOR ORDERED

It's been a hot day. The Fremantle Doctor* has arrived and the sun is on its way down to kiss the ocean. Plastered with sunscreen, sand and salt, and wondering whether you've got heat stroke, you're tired and hungry but really can't be bothered changing out of your beachwear. Fear not! A great meal and a refreshing glass of wine requires no more effort than slipping on a pair of thongs, throwing on a sarong and walking up the sand dune to Clancy's, where a sign over the door reads, 'Sandy feet and thongs welcome'.

Sitting on an endless stretch of pristine sand, this casual but funky eatery has embraced the beach with colourful and humorous style. Towels have been woven into chandeliers, and thongs, buckets and spades adorn doorways. Lined up in front of the glassed balcony overlooking the beach are colourful 1950s-style wooden beach chairs. Make new friends at a long table or perch on a bar stool with views across to the sparkling sea.

There's a great range of local beers and ciders on tap, and the food is some of the best pub grub around. Fish of the day, oysters Kilpatrick* and mussels with lemon and butter will definitely impress, but the best value for money is Clancy's beer-battered fish, chips and homemade coleslaw. Red-meat lovers can also get an excellent feed with the rib-eye steak or kangaroo fillet, and even vegetarians get a say with the delicious goat's-cheese tart.

Best of all is the service: the young and cheerful staff will have you forgetting about your heat stroke – and all that sand stuck in uncomfortable places – in no time.

> FEELING PECKISH?

195 Challenger Pde, City Beach
(08) 9385 7555
www.clancysfishpub.com.au
Open Mon–Fri 12pm–late,
Sat–Sun 9am–late

See also
map 1 A2

'ENCYCLO' TRIVIA

* The Fremantle Doctor is what locals call the cooling sea breeze that rolls in on summer afternoons, bringing welcome relief from the heat.

* Oysters Kilpatrick are oysters dressed up with bacon and Worcestershire sauce.

BLUE-JEAN CUISINE

You didn't hear it from us, but mark our words: cafes are the future for food. While MasterChef contestants chase fame and book deals, the cooking game's journeymen and women are swapping their spiffy chef whites for an apron, a pair of jeans and a T-shirt.

Graeme Shapiro at Fremantle's Wild Poppy is a case in point. Once upon a dinnertime, chef Shapiro plied his trade in the credit-card singeing world of fine dining, but for this, the next stage of his career, it's all about serving honest, Asian-influenced cooking in casual surrounds (think couches aplenty and bright, subtly kitsch decor). No matter what time of day it is, there's always something on the menu that appeals: a cheddar-and-spring-onion waffle with bacon and herbed ricotta, say, or maybe a wok-fried crab omelette. And that's just breakfast.

The lunchtime menu ups the ante, with dishes such as banh mi* – made with love and shaped by his travels to Vietnam, Shapiro's version is a thing of porky beauty. Dinner raises the bar another level again, with the likes of fish curry and a Thai-style pork-and-peanut sausage beckoning diners.

In a locality where every second shopfront seems to be a casual eatery of sorts, it's no mean feat that Wild Poppy has quickly established itself as a detour worth taking. That might be because it's in a quieter part of town away from the port city's established strip, but chef Shapiro's kitchen mastery has more than just a little to do with this cosy corner cafe's appeal – that, and the fact that he looks great in denim.

> FEELING PECKISH?

2 Wray Ave, Fremantle
(08) 9430 8555
Open Mon–Thurs 7am–4pm, Fri–Sat
7am–4pm & 6–10pm, Sun 8am–4pm

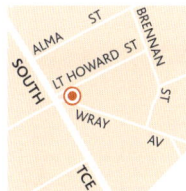

See also
map 2 B5

'ENCYCLO' TRIVIA

* Banh mi are Vietnam's legendary pork baguettes. While every banh mi vendor in Vietnam will have their own recipe, pork, carrot, coriander, chilli and pâté are the defining ingredients of this amazing roll.

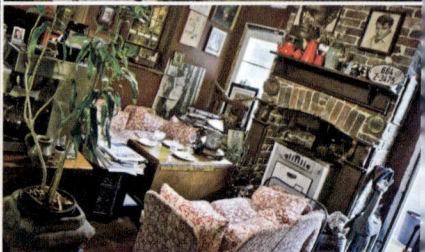

> FEELING PECKISH?

CAFE MUELLER

THE GERMANY YOU NEVER KNEW EXISTED

It's perhaps best to begin this review with a small disclaimer: you will *never* forget your first visit to Cafe Mueller. To describe this restaurant as unconventional is a wee bit of an understatement. Unlike so many of Perth's run-of-the-mill, overpriced and underwhelming eateries, this kooky bric-a-brac bolthole is well and truly a sanctuary from the norm.

An evening here is one spent in another (slightly warped) century – one where Marlene Dietrich rules the gramophone, surrealist art commands every inch of wall space* and the schnapps is poured liberally. A long-time culinary institution of the eastern suburbs, Cafe Mueller shut up shop for going on a decade, before reopening for business in 2009. And thankfully little has changed.

Owned and run by the somewhat eccentric German émigré Karl Mueller and his partner Len, Cafe Mueller is a menu-free zone (and fully BYO). An ode to simplicity, there are no tongue-twisting appetisers here – you simply enjoy whatever Karl's cooked up that evening, while taking in the unforgettable sights and sounds. Unfussy country German fare, the meals are graciously uncomplicated – soup for entrée (complemented by Karl's warm homemade rye bread) and grilled or roasted meats for main, served with greens and warm potato salad. There's not a boiled pork knuckle or lump of sauerkraut in sight!

The only decision you need to make all night is whether to have the baked German cheesecake or Black Forest ice-cream for dessert. With three courses coming in at under $35 a head, taking a walk on the wild and crazy German side couldn't be more appealing.

> FEELING PECKISH?

12 William St, Midland
(08) 9250 1661
Open Thurs–Sun 6.30pm–12am

See also
map 3 D2

'ENCYCLO' TRIVIA

* Feel free to make an offer for the art on display, and you can also check out the owners' own handy work in the studio out the back.

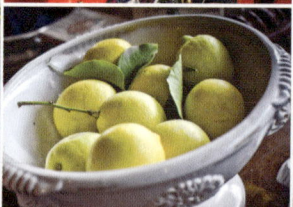

IT'S A FAMILY AFFAIR

Is it wrong to eat only cake for lunch? Boucla owner Despina Tanner wouldn't think so. Up at the crack of dawn baking, Despina exudes warmth and generosity – you get the impression she'd be baking in the wee hours regardless of whether she ran a cafe or not. She set out to make Boucla a destination, and, given her Greek background and the menu, you'd be forgiven for thinking you'd been washed up on some Greek island like Kastellorizo, where her family originated.

But back to that cake. It's a tough call between a huge slice of the one bursting with apples, sultanas and spice, and the extra-special chocolate-and-ricotta cake. If guilt gets the better of you, you won't be disappointed with the savoury provincial food on offer. It's rustic through and through, from the chunky gourmet salads glistening with crispness, to the mezze plates and lip-smacking baklava (best downed with a burst of intense coffee), all complemented by the mismatched cushions, Turkish rug and black-and-white family photos on the walls. The cafe's compact size and popularity ensure it's always buzzing. Don't worry about whether you'll ever find a seat: somehow everyone gets seated, even if it means being tacked onto an already occupied table.

This is a family affair. Despina's children float in and out, her husband's artwork adorns the walls – although he's just as famous for his soups – and the memory of Despina's father, a Rokeby Road local from way back, lingers. As a 'boucla' is a round decorative brooch, the circular symbolism is perfect: the cafe clasps this family circle – and its circle of friends in the community – together.

> FEELING PECKISH?

349 Rokeby Rd, Subiaco
(08) 9381 2841
www.boucla.com
Open Mon–Wed & Fri 7am–5pm,
Sat 7am–3.30pm, Thurs 7am–5pm &
6–9.30pm

See also
map 1 B5

> FEELING PECKISH?

THE FULL KIT AND KABUKI

Welcome to the inner-city canteen for CBD workers desperately holding out till payday: at Taka's Kitchen, all bar the large sashimi combination is a tenner or less. Not that its bargain-priced menu is strictly for the budget-conscious – the only prerequisite needed to feast here is a willingness to wait in line and possibly share dining space with strangers on communal tables.

For some, the experience is nothing more than a pit stop for takeaway sushi (both rolls and nigiri* are available), however, the full kit and kabuki is best experienced dining in. As canny lunch buddies prove time after time, the best plan of attack is to eat with a friend – that way one of you can shotgun some seats while the other joins the ever-present queue and orders.

After you've paid (cash only), staff will give you an electronic beeper that buzzes and flashes when it's your turn to collect, but until then you'll have to enviously eye off plates of crisp tori kara-age (Japanese fried chicken), comforting katsudon (crumbed and deep-fried pork cutlets with egg on rice) and bowls of tempura udon (deep-fried battered seafood and vegetables with noodles) being devoured with relish around you. As well as the obligatory Japanese condiments such as wasabi and soy, guests can help themselves to free green tea from the metal urn.

How Taka's has stayed afloat all these years is anyone's guess, but as long as it continues to deliver the cheap and the cheerful, the ravenous will continue to clog Shafto Lane.

> FEELING PECKISH?

Shops 5 & 6, Shafto La, Perth
(08) 9324 1234
www.takaskitchen.iinet.net.au
Open Mon–Sat 11am–9pm,
Sun 11am–5pm

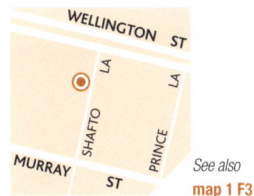

See also
map 1 F3

'ENCYCLO' TRIVIA

* In contrast to sushi rolls, where meat and seafood are wrapped in rice and seaweed, nigiri sushi toppings are pressed onto rectangles of rice.

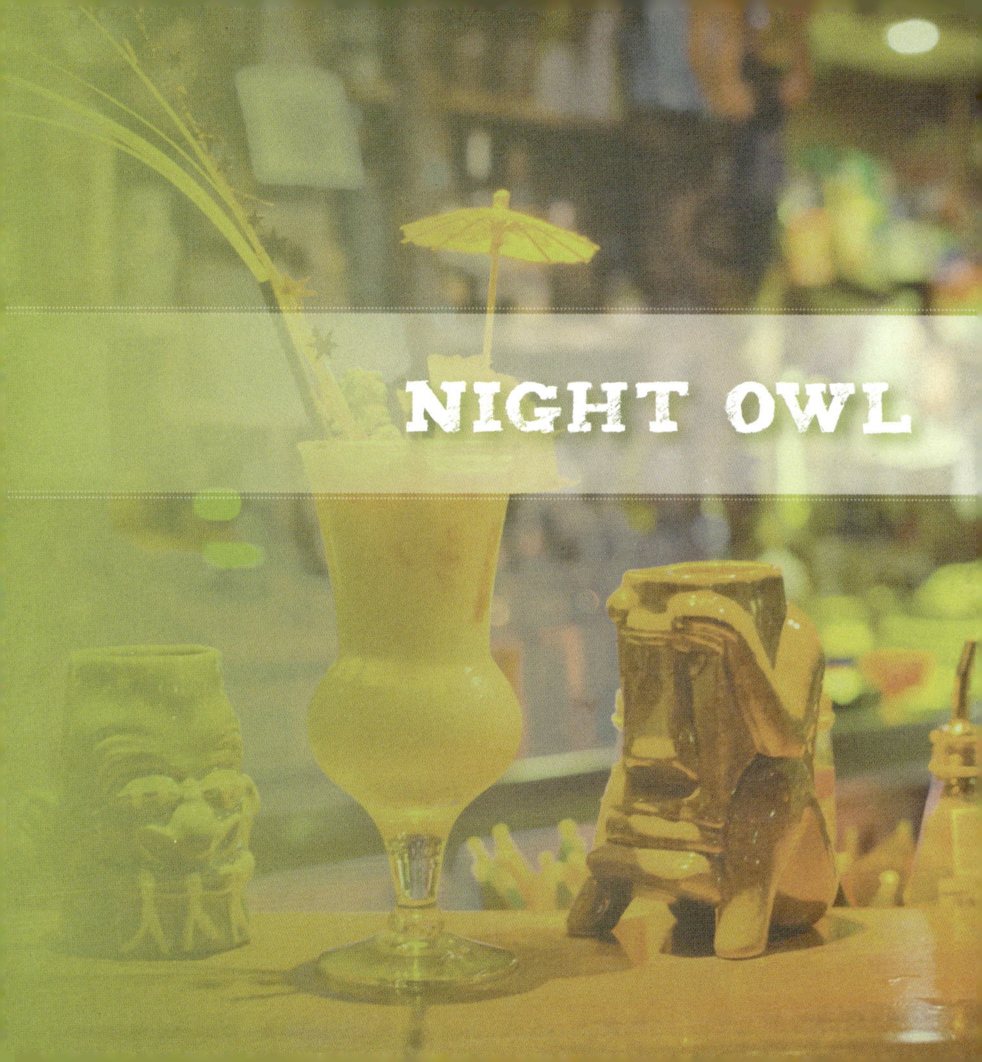

NIGHT OWL

DEVILLES PAD

HEAVEN CAN WAIT

Sometimes fun is found in the unlikeliest of places. Take the railway end of Aberdeen Street and its surrounds. Distinguished by its drab semi-industrial vibe and a disproportionate number of churches, the area doesn't exactly scream excitement. But for night owls in the know, this end of town is a hotbed of Las Vegas–style sizzle. Get your glamour on, darlin': we're going to Devilles Pad.

Equal parts live-music venue, burlesque den, sinful Southern diner and go-go-tastic nightclub, Devilles Pad is a nightspot like no other. It may not look like much from outside, but inside's a whole different story. Blending lurid 1960s B-film aesthetics with lashings of demonic kitsch, this is what hell might've looked like if imagined by Mario Bava circa *Danger: Diabolik**. Red lighting sets the mood, while larger-than-life statues of voluptuous succubi* and 'molten' rock walls heighten the effect. Grab a booth and feast on snacks such as Evil Empanadas and Hellapeno Poppers, or flirt with eternal damnation as you quaff a killer cocktail or three (Horny Devil, anyone?). It's all wholesome, tongue-in-cheek fun, of course.

Like they say, no rest for the wicked – you'll be shaking it on the sunken dance floor with the other sinners before the evening's out. Whether it's an Elvis tribute band or a '60s beat combo, a magician or a go-go troupe, the live acts are always jumping, as are the in-house DJs, spinning the coolest vintage sounds in town from their custom-built grotto. Check the website for details of Devilles' famed theme nights, where anything from *Batman* to *Mad Men* goes.

Never has a night out been so diabolically entertaining.

> NIGHT OWL

3 Aberdeen St, East Perth
(08) 9225 6669
www.devillespad.com
Open Thurs 6pm–12am, Fri 5pm–2am,
Sat 6pm–2am

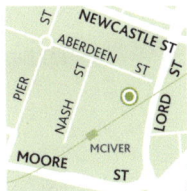

See also
map 1 H3

'ENCYCLO' TRIVIA

* Perhaps the swinging-est film of the 1960s, *Danger: Diabolik* is a high-spirited pop-art romp by Italian director Mario Bava, in which the hero lives in a psychedelic underground hideout not unlike Devilles Pad.

* A succubus is a female demon that likes to have sex with men while they're asleep …

LAZY SUSAN'S COMEDY DEN

LAZY SUSAN'S COMEDY DEN

A LAUGH A MINUTE

An Englishman, an Irishman and a Scotsman walk into a bar … Come on now, work with me on this one. Said Englishman, Irishman and Scotsman decide to climb the stairs, where they discover Lazy Susan's Comedy Den, Perth's definitive home of gags.

A cult institution among Perth's comedy fraternity, Lazy Susan's has been dishing out belly laughs for years. A toasty little theatre where giggles are on tap and poured cheaply, it serves up the best in local and interstate comic talent night after night, upstairs at the Brisbane Hotel. And, the funny thing is, if you're not a comedy regular, you've probably never heard of it. So while we have the microphone, let's fill you in!

Dedicated to original comedy that's accessible but at the forefront of the genre, every evening offers something wildly diverse. On Tuesdays it's all about experimental comedy, where first-timers and old hands road test new material. Thursdays boast a monthly puppet extravaganza (adults only, of course, so leave the kiddies at home), Fridays are stand-up heaven, and Saturdays are all about the Big HooHaa, an evening of improvised comedy and theatre sports where two teams battle it out for comedic supremacy, and where madness is not only welcomed but encouraged.

There's no tonic quite like laughter, so if it's a fix of the funnies you're after, Lazy Susan's is the place to get your fill. Now, back to that Englishman, Irishman and Scotsman …

> NIGHT OWL

Level 1, 292 Beaufort St, Highgate
(08) 9328 2543
www.lazysusans.com.au
Open Tues & Thurs–Sat 8pm–12am

See also
map 1 H2

THE JAZZ CELLAR

FOLLOW YOUR EARS

You expect to discover hidden places in a book like this, but so tucked away is the Jazz Cellar, I wasn't sure I was even close to finding it until I stood still and heard faint strains of Dixieland floating out into the night.

Fifteen years ago the Corner House Jazz Band was looking for a venue and discovered a hole underneath the floor of an old building they owned. They dug it out and the Jazz Cellar was born. Inspired by the film *Some Like it Hot**, the club's very secret entrance is behind this building (currently a Salvation Army op shop), down an alley and through an old English telephone box.

It's the only venue in Perth dedicated to traditional and Dixieland jazz, and in keeping with its vintage musical heritage it clings determinedly to an old-fashioned ambience and hospitality. The walls are decorated with old posters advertising everything from cigarettes to soap powder, and the chairs and tables are a mishmash of materials, shapes and sizes.

This fabulous time warp is only open on Friday nights; $20 will get you in and it's BYO food and booze. It fits 100 people and those 100 squeeze in for dear life, bringing supper and their tipple of choice and filling the cellar with laughter, cheerful banter and up-close-and-personal dancing. It's a family atmosphere, where kids, parents and grandparents share the fun of trad jazz, and regulars get up and sing a set.

The band kicks off at 7.30pm, but patrons start arriving just after 5pm to get a table; by the time the music starts, the 'full house' sign is up. So don't be late – and remember to bring a plate.

> **NIGHT OWL**

Cnr Scarborough Beach Rd & Buxton St, Mt Hawthorn
(08) 9447 8111
Open Fri 5.30–10.30pm

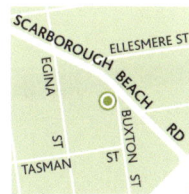

See also **map 1 D1**

'ENCYCLO' TRIVIA

* The 1959 American comedy *Some Like it Hot*, starring Jack Lemmon, Tony Curtis and Marilyn Monroe, is regarded as one of the finest films ever made. The idea for a secret jazz club came from the film's opening scenes, where a funeral parlour is a front for a speakeasy during the 1920s prohibition era in Chicago.

> NIGHT OWL

THE BAKERY

COOKING WITH NOISE

For far too long Perth's live-music landscape had a mighty gaping hole. While well quenched with suitable small bar rooms and larger concert spaces, the city lacked a medium-sized venue dedicated to music and music alone. Enter the Bakery.

The brainchild of the creative folk at Artrage – Western Australia's not-for-profit arts collective – the Bakery finally reopened in its present incarnation in 2010, much to the cheer of local and touring bands tired of being left with little option but to play unsuitable stages.

But a simple stage and band room this is not. The Bakery is, by design, an experience: a deconstructionist utopia of recycled sea containers and cavernous spaces. And the main band room is one of the finest in town, engineered with the musician and punter in mind – indeed, you can actually see the band from wherever in the room you may choose to tap your loafers!

The venue's programming also sets it apart from the pack. While the state's musical pedigree is well established, the Bakery errs on the distant frontier of unpredictability, courting the obtuse over the mainstream. Austere, Teutonic* beats? Check. Fuzzed-out, mind-bending psychedelia? Check. Twelve-tone minimalist electronica? Check. The Bakery's unofficial motto is 'the stranger the lovelier'; it's a fiefdom of aural freedom, dedicated unreservedly to the art of noise. Oh, and it does book the odd 'normal' band too.

So get your freak on and fire the ovens … it's time to bake!

> NIGHT OWL

233 James St, Northbridge
(08) 9227 6288
www.nowbaking.com.au
Open Fri–Sat 8pm–2am, Sun 7pm–12am

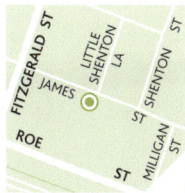

See also
map 1 F3

'ENCYCLO' TRIVIA

* The Teutons were a tribe that lived in what is today modern Germany, and are responsible for much of that country's contemporary language and culture.

HULA BULA BAR

SET SAIL FOR A RUM-KISSED COCKTAIL

What's your idea of paradise? If it involves lush tropical islands, blazing Polynesian sunsets and potent, rum-kissed cocktails, then set sail for the Hula Bula Bar now. Granted, it's not actually on a beach, but this exotic little tiki den in the heart of the CBD will awaken your inner castaway faster than you can say, 'Make mine a Mai Tai, cap'n'.

Step inside and find yourself in a Pacific island wonderland of glowering tiki gods and hula maidens, cosy tiger-print booths and enough ferns to make you forget the concrete jungle outside. Presiding over this colourful oasis is an elaborately hand-carved bamboo bar straight out of a Shag* painting. Think that's impressive? Wait till you taste the cocktails.

Forget Fluffy Ducks: these babies are the real deal, part of a proud tradition dating back to the glory days of Trader Vic's and Don the Beachcomber*. Mixed with panache and garnished with flair, classics like Mar Tikis, Shrunken Heads and Piña Coladas will quench the most demanding thirst. Some cocktails are even served in eye-popping tiki mugs for that extra-authentic touch. True to tropical form, rum features heavily – Hula Bula stocks varieties rarely found this far south of the Caribbean. It even hosts a monthly rum club for aficionados.

Of course, cocktails always taste better with a 'groovy' musical chaser, especially one bursting with tunes from those tiki-friendly eras, the '50s, '60s and '70s. Depending on when you're there, you could hear anything from vintage calypso to greasy funk, primitive rock'n'roll to country twang. Hula Bula's discerning DJs know how to keep the luau* humming.

Who needs the expense of a Hawaiian holiday? Say aloha to the Hula Bula Bar!

> NIGHT OWL

12 Victoria Ave, Perth
(08) 9225 4457
www.hulabulabar.com
Open Wed–Thurs 4pm–12am,
Fri 4pm–1am, Sat 6pm–1am

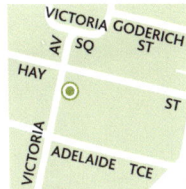

VICTORIA GODERICH
AV SQ ST
HAY
ST
VICTORIA
ADELAIDE TCE

*See also
map 1 H4*

'ENCYCLO' TRIVIA

* Shag (aka Josh Agle) is a contemporary Californian artist with his heart in the past. His brightly coloured paintings and prints evoke a time when sharply dressed men and ultra-chic women partied in tiki bars and modernist lounge rooms.

* Trader Vic's and Don the Beachcomber were two of the first Polynesian-themed bars in the US: the former opened in 1934, the latter a few years later. Legions of imitators followed and tiki mania was born.

* A luau is a party, Hawaiian-style.

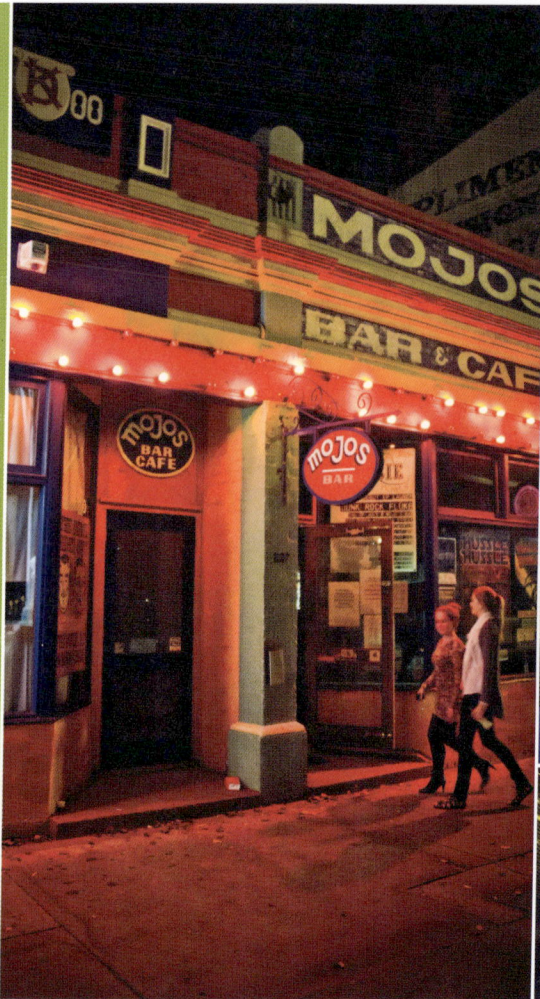

WE LIKE THAT OLD-TIME ROCK'N'ROLL

Western Australia rocks – and we're not talking about those precious metals that litter the soil of this fair state. Responsible for some of Australia's greatest contemporary musical talent, this golden city is home to, among other luminaries, John Butler Trio, Empire of the Sun, Jebediah, Eskimo Joe, The Waifs, The Sleepy Jackson and Tame Impala. Aside from being sandgropers, these bands all have another thing in common – they've all played Mojo's Bar.

Perth's very own CBGB*-style original music joint, Mojo's is unlike any other live-music venue in town – wholeheartedly dedicated to life's ultimate aural elixir, it's intimate and unconcerned with fad. On any given night of the week you're quite likely to stumble upon your brand-new favourite band, whether they be hard rock, folk, blues, reggae, hip hop or electro. Literally anything goes at Mojo's, seven nights a week – including a regular Monday open-mic night, if you fancy yourself a contender.

Situated on the emerging entertainment strip of Queen Victoria Street – heading up a trilogy of live venues within stage-diving distance, including The Swan and The Railway hotels – Mojo's intimate band room is cosy but inspired, with a lengthy stretch of bar that makes getting a refill of the local ale a breeze. And if tonight's grindcore* band ain't your thing, there's always the courtyard to escape to, where you can chill to sultry summer grooves under Freo's moonlight. And what's a rock'n'roll bar without a beer-stained pool table? Indeed, Mojo's is the real deal.

> NIGHT OWL

237 Queen Victoria St, North Fremantle
(08) 9430 4010
www.mojosbar.com.au
Open Mon–Sun 6pm–late

See also
map 2 B3

'ENCYCLO' TRIVIA

* CBGB was founded in 1973 as a home of 'country, blue grass and blues', but soon became New York's pre-eminent punk and underground rock'n'roll club.

* Grindcore is an extreme branch of hard-metal music born in England in the 1980s, and categorised by its breakneck speed, tuned-down guitars and primal vocal growls.

KITSCH BAR

ONE NIGHT IN BANGKOK

Like a bustling night market in a busy Asian city, a visit to Kitsch Bar tantalises the senses, turning a night out in suburban Leederville into an exotic adventure. The open-plan kitchen of this small bar-cum-restaurant lures folks in off the street with the intoxicating aroma of Asian cuisine. After a few drinks and an entrée or three, it really starts to feel like your Asian home away from home.

Indeed, with mismatched furniture, vintage lamps and quirky art aplenty, this Leederville local resembles a cool friend's share house. But instead of grumpy housemates, a dirty bathroom and a sink full of dishes, Kitsch provides waiters who treat you like long-lost family, amazing beverages and a cheap-and-cheerful menu that won't break the bank.

After walking through the oriental gate and down the wooden ramp, above which paper lanterns sway in the breeze, your every whim and desire will be catered to – so long as those whims and desires involve mouth-watering morsels, fruity cocktails and icy-cold brews. Though the food menu is rather short, the drinks list more than makes up for it, with enough beers, wines and cocktails to slake any thirst. After downing a few glasses your appetite will be piqued and ready to share modern takes on classic Asian dishes, such as sesame prawn toast with plum-lime ponzu* and deep-fried salt-and-pepper tofu with hoisin*. Yum!

A place where you can kick off your shoes and put your feet up in summer, or nestle under a blanket with friends in winter, Kitsch is a little slice of Asia in the heart of Perth. Let the adventure begin!

> **NIGHT OWL**

229 Oxford St, Leederville
(08) 9242 1229
www.kitschbar.com.au
Open Tues 5–10.30pm,
Wed–Sat 5pm–12am

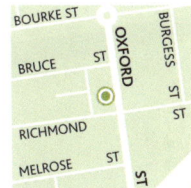

BOURKE ST
BRUCE ST
OXFORD
BURGESS
RICHMOND ST
MELROSE ST

See also
map1 D1

'ENCYCLO' TRIVIA

* Ponzu is a tart but tasty Japanese citrus-based sauce.

* A delicious, dark-red, sweet and spicy dipping sauce, hoisin is made from soybeans, and is the perfect accompaniment to a salty Asian entrée.

HELVETICA

SLICK AMBER POUR

For most people, the word Helvetica means one of two things: either the Latin name for fence-sitting nation extraordinaire Switzerland*, or a sans-serif font that, despite its versatility, you're frankly sick of seeing everywhere. For the good folk of Perth, it has a third meaning, that being the name of the city's fairest and best of the current small-bar population.

As you'd expect, grog is one of Helvetica's strong points, and while the stocks of this contemporary speakeasy run deep across every level of the booze pyramid, it's whisk(e)y* that sits at its base. From familiar names such as Glenfiddich and Jack (as in Daniel's, although it's likely to be the more superior Single Barrel Tennessee version than the ubiquitous black-labelled bottles) to the thrillingly obscure, including bottles lovingly hand-carried back to Australia from all corners of the world, Helvetica's blood runs amber.

But it's not all cocktails and peat'n'neat*: carefully chosen beers and wine are always available, while impressive food offerings round off the experience, particularly if you've managed to score a table in the recently opened upstairs lounge, where guests enjoy table service and the ability to order snacks from an extended menu.

We're big fans of the fit out too: the combination of timber, exposed brick, slick lines (and even slicker staff) creates a welcoming, lived-in feel. Odds are that, with time, Helvetica will come to mean a favourite drinking hole for you too.

> NIGHT OWL

101 St Georges Tce, Perth
(enter via Howard La)
(08) 9321 4422
www.helveticabar.com
Open Tues–Thurs 3pm–12am,
Fri 12pm–12am, Sat 6pm–12am

See also
map 1 G4

'ENCYCLO' TRIVIA

* Once upon a time Switzerland was known as Confoederatio Helvetica, a part of history referenced by the country's EU abbreviation, CH.

* Whisk(e)y: do you spell it with an 'e' or without? The answer, my budding boozehound, is in the country of origin. If it's Scottish, it's 'whisky' while the Irish (and most American distillers) spell it 'whiskey'. Other countries are free to choose whichever spelling they like.

* Peat'n'neat is a term we've come up with: the peat refers to the smoky peaty character found in many whiskies, while neat is a nod to the purist's preferred method of consumption.

SUGAR BLUE BURLESQUE

YOU CAN LEAVE YOUR HAT ON

Often confused with striptease, the art of burlesque is actually just about the tease, with fluttering eyelashes, the curve of a breast and the allure of what lies beneath your corset. It's glorious glamour from a bygone era, combining dance, comedy, music and theatre in one. And it's yours for the taking at Sugar Blue Burlesque, a performance troupe and burlesque academy.

Sugar Blue classes cater for all tastes and talents, from gentle introductions and casual drop-in 'bump-and-grind' sessions, to themes like the 1920s, Latin, cabaret, go-go dancing, showgirl and hula hooping. The heart-racing advanced courses take you to the next level with the use of props likes chairs and feathers, combined with audience interaction and costume making.

If you prefer to save your charms for a private audience, then leave it to the professionals, who have a busy dance card year round with shows and performances all over town. The Sugar Blue troupe also offers tasteful entertainment services sure to spice up any function, including fundraisers, corporate events and hens' nights – where many a bride-to-be has received saucy wedding-night tips …

Pick up some nipple tassels at a retro market or go the whole sexy-siren look by attending one of the academy's vintage-glamour workshops, which include a professional photo shoot (for lasting proof of your pin-up-girl potential).

So go on, don your feathers, fan and suspenders, channel your best inner Mae West, and shout from the rooftops, 'Hey big spender!'

> NIGHT OWL

**Headquarters at Burlesque Lounge,
Level 1, 267 William St, Northbridge
0413 661 027
www.theburlesquelounge.com
See website for class times and locations**

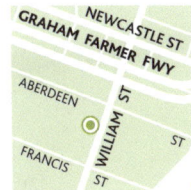

See also
map 1 G3

## THE SUITE

A SUPER SUBI SPECIAL

While the recent small-bar renaissance has changed the way the inner city drinks, it's still very much a case of same-old, same-old in the 'burbs. Unless, that is, the 'hood you happen to be in is Subiaco. Poky yet perky, the Suite not only provides locals with an intimate venue to get their good times on, but it could well gift the rest of the metropolitan area with a blueprint from which to mint their own neighbourhood hang-outs.

Visually, there's more than a touch of cafe-dom to the Suite, with tables, couches and low-back banquettes dotting the wood-heavy, bar-at-the-back interior. No biggie – all the better to put your feet up and enjoy the table service, my dear. Linen napkins* to go with your roast-vegetable-and-quinoa salad or Spencers Brook* sausages in sugo are another example of the above-and-beyond measures the Suite goes to in the name of pleasing its clientele.

Of course, one cannot survive on food alone, and, as you'd expect, the beer, wine and cocktail selections have been chosen with care to ensure hydration is both enjoyable and essential. While the bartenders have obviously been given room to stretch their legs (iced Irish coffee!), they also pay attention to the classics and have the skills and liquor-cabinet fodder to mix the best of them.

Garnish the lot with smart friendly service, value-packed drink specials – between 4pm and 7pm Tuesday to Sunday, cocktails can be enjoyed at the budget-friendly price of just $11 – and a vibe that's both high class yet down to earth, and you've got a local haunt with appeal extending way beyond its suburban boundaries.

> NIGHT OWL

210 Nicholson Rd, Subiaco
(08) 9381 2170
www.darkhorsedevelopments.com.au
Open Tues–Fri 7am–12am, Sat
8am–12am, Sun 8am–9pm

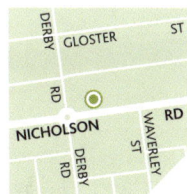

See also
map 1 A5

'ENCYCLO' TRIVIA

* Re those linen napkins: so long as dishes like this keep coming, we wouldn't care if we had to wipe our hands on our jeans.

* Spencers Brook is a farm located 90 km east of Perth in the district of the same name. All its products come from free-range pigs that are reared with consideration for the animals' welfare.

091

MY OWN PERTH DISCOVERIES

PHOTOGRAPHY CREDITS

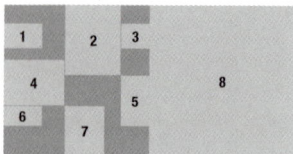

HIT THE STREETS

1 Courtesy of Museum of Performing Arts
2–5 Erika Budiman
6 Courtesy of Macc Coffee Bar
7 Courtesy of Blue Room Theatre
8 Courtesy of Breastique Art

THE BLUE ROOM THEATRE

Photos courtesy of the Blue Room Theatre

RIVERSIDE AT WOODBRIDGE

Photos by Erika Budiman

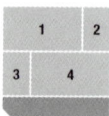

BREASTIQUE ART

Photos by Carmen Jenner

VENN

1 & 3–4 Courtesy of VENN
2 Erika Budiman

BON SCOTT PILGRIMAGE

Photos by Erika Budiman

MACC COFFEE BAR & EVENTS

Photos by Melissa Krafchek

DR SNIPPY'S BARBER LOUNGE

1–2 Erika Budiman
3 Clint Ariti

MUSEUM OF PERFORMING ARTS

Photos courtesy of Museum of Performing Arts

PERTH CITY FARM

1–3, 5–6 & 8 Erika Budiman
4 & 7 Jeff Atkinson

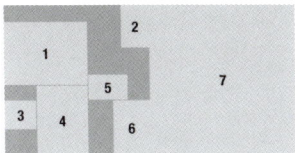

TREASURE TROVE

1, 4, 5 & 7 Erika Budiman
2 & 3 Melissa Krafchek
6 Photography by Robyn Louise Photography;
modelling by Janiielle Rodriguez

PIGEONHOLE

1–3 Erika Budiman
4–6 Melissa Krafchek

OH HENRY! VINTAGE

Photos by Melissa Krafchek

WILLIAM TOPP

1. & 6. Melissa Krafchek
2.–5. & 7. Erika Budiman

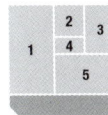

TEA FOR ME

1 & 3–5 Erika Budiman
2 Melissa Krafchek

YO YO BUFFALO

Photos by Erika Budiman

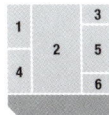

MR SPARROW

1, 3 & 6 Melissa Krafchek
2 Courtesy of Mr Sparrow
4–5 Erika Budiman

THE PEARL OF HIGHGATE

Photos by Erika Budiman

BEYOND SKATE

Photos by Joel Dunbar & Luke Thompson

RED DUSK DESIGNS

1 Photography by Robyn Louise Photography; modelling by
Janiielle Rodriguez
2 Photography by Marita Bird Photography; make-up by Kylie
Trolove; hair by Jesse Blue; modelling by Marijke Loosjes
3 Photography by Silver Bullet Photography; make-up by
Sandy Tau; hair by Hair at Guildford; modelling Daryll Satie

NELL'S EMPORIUM

1 Emma Bergmeier
2–7 Erika Budiman

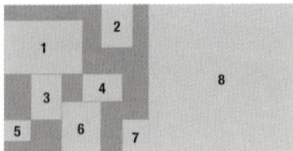

FEELING PECKISH?

1, 3–6 & 8 Erika Budiman
2 & 7 Melissa Krafchek

PONY EXPRESS O

Photos by Erika Budiman

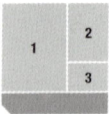

TONG86

Photos by Erika Budiman

ALFRED'S KITCHEN

Photos by Erika Budiman

TOAST

Photos by Erika Budiman

GOOD ONE BBQ RESTAURANT

1 Erika Budiman
2–3 Melissa Krafchek

CABIN FEVER

1–4 Erika Budiman
5 Melissa Krafchek

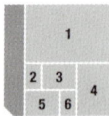

CLANCY'S FISH PUB

1, 2 & 4–6 Erika Budiman
3 & 5 Courtesy of Clancy's Fish Pub

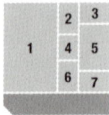

WILD POPPY

1–2 & 4–7 Melissa Krafchek
3 Erika Budiman

CAFE MUELLER

Photos by Erika Budiman

BOUCLA

1, 3–4 & 6–7 Erika Budiman
2 & 5 Melissa Krafchek

TAKA'S KITCHEN

1 Erika Budiman
2–5 Melissa Krafchek

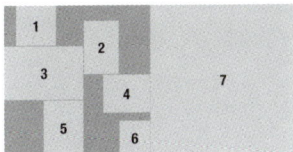

NIGHT OWL

1, 3–5 & 7 Erika Budiman
2 Daniel Khoo
6 Jamie Syme

DEVILLES PAD

1–2 & 4 Johnny Trask
3 Daniel Khoo

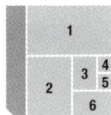

LAZY SUSAN'S COMEDY DEN

1 Andrew Bell
2 & 4–6 Erika Budiman
3 Melissa Krafchek

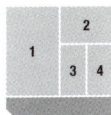

THE JAZZ CELLAR

1 Erika Budiman
2–4 Melissa Krafchek

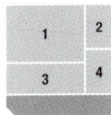

THE BAKERY

1, 2 & 4 Erika Budiman
3 Courtesy of the Bakery

HULA BULA BAR

Photos by Erika Budiman

MOJO'S BAR

Photos by Erika Budiman

KITSCH BAR

Photos by Jamie Syme

HELVETICA

Photos courtesy of Helvetica

SUGAR BLUE BURLESQUE

Photos by Erika Budiman

THE SUITE

1–2 & 4 Courtesy of the Suite
3 & 5 Erika Budiman

ACKNOWLEDGEMENTS

The publisher would like to acknowledge the following individuals and organisations:

Publications manager: Astrid Browne

Project manager: Melissa Krafchek

Editor: Michelle Bennett

Design and photo selection: Erika Budiman

Writers: Julian Tompkin, Emma Bergmeier, Max Veenhuyzen, Carmen Jenner, Sarah McNeill, Sam Wilson

Cartography: Emily Maffei, Bruce McGurty, Paul de Leur

Pre-press: PageSet Digital Print & Pre-press

PHOTOGRAPHY CREDITS

Cover (clockwise from main image):
Going, Going ... Gone! ice-cream sculpture by Stuart Clipston as part of Sculpture by the Sea, Cottesloe (Photo: www.louisebeaumont.com); Graffiti at Perth City Farm, East Perth (Erika Budiman); Performer at Sugar Blue Burlesque, Northbridge (Erika Budiman); Skateboards display at Beyond Skate, Perth CBD (Joel Dunbar & Luke Thompson); Barbecuing meat at Tong86, Northbridge (Erika Budiman)

Back cover:
Mural outside Wild Poppy, Fremantle (Erika Budiman)

Half-title page:
Mural in a passageway in Perth's CBD (Erika Budiman)

Title pages:
Dining room at Clancy's Fish Pub, City Beach (Erika Budiman)

About this guide:
Deckchairs at Clancy's Fish Pub, City Beach (Erika Budiman)

Explore Australia Publishing Pty Ltd
Ground Floor, Building 1, 658 Church Street, Richmond, VIC 3121

Explore Australia Publishing Pty Ltd is a division of Hardie Grant Publishing Pty Ltd

hardie grant publishing

Published by Explore Australia Publishing Pty Ltd, 2011

Concept, text, maps, form and design © Explore Australia Publishing Pty Ltd, 2011

The maps in this publication incorporate data © Commonwealth of Australia (Geoscience Australia), 2006. Geoscience Australia has not evaluated the data as altered and incorporated within this publication, and therefore gives no warranty regarding accuracy, reliability, currency or suitability for any particular purpose.

Inside front and back cover maps © Imprint and currency – VAR Product and PSMA Data

"Copyright. Based on data provided under licence from PSMA Australia Limited (www.psma.com.au)".

Hydrography Data (May 2006)
Parks & Reserves Data (May 2006)
Transport Data (February 2011)

DISCLAIMER

While every care is taken to ensure the accuracy of the data within this product, the owners of the data (including the state, territory and Commonwealth governments of Australia) do not make any representations or warranties about its accuracy, reliability, completeness or suitability for any particular purpose and, to the extent permitted by law, the owners of the data disclaim all responsibility and all liability (including without limitation, liability in negligence) for all expenses, losses, damages, (including indirect or consequential damages) and costs which might be incurred as a result of the data being inaccurate or incomplete in any way and for any reason.

ISBN 9781741173703

10 9 8 7 6 5 4 3 2 1

Printed and bound in China by 1010 Printing International Ltd

Publisher's note: Every effort has been made to ensure that the information in this book is accurate at the time of going to press. The publisher welcomes information and suggestions for correction or improvement. Email: info@exploreaustralia.net.au

Publisher's disclaimers: The publisher cannot accept responsibility for any errors or omissions. The representation on the maps of any road or track is not necessarily evidence of public right of way. The publisher cannot be held responsible for any injury, loss or damage incurred during travel. It is vital to research any proposed trip thoroughly and seek the advice of relevant state and travel organisations before you leave.